THE HOME PATTERN COMPANY
1914 Fashions Catalog

The Home Pattern Company
with a New Introduction by Kristina Harris

DOVER PUBLICATIONS, INC.
New York

Bibliographical Note

The Home Pattern Company 1914 Fashions Catalog, first published by Dover Publications, Inc., in 1995, is an unabridged republication of *The Home Book of Fashions, Winter 1914, Volume 1, Number 2*, originally published by The Home Pattern Company, New York, in 1914. The illustrations appearing in color in the original are here reproduced in black and white. A new Introduction has been written specially for the Dover edition by Kristina Harris.

Library of Congress Cataloging-in-Publication Data

The Home Pattern Company 1914 fashions catalog / the Home Pattern Company ; new introduction by Kristina Harris.
    p.   cm.
  Reprint. Originally published 1914 under title: The Home book of fashions. Winter 1914, Volume 1, Number 2.
  ISBN 0-486-28688-6 (pbk.)
  1. Dressmaking—Patterns—Catalogs. 2. Tailoring—Patterns—Catalogs. 3. Fashion—History—20th century. I. Harris, Kristina. II. Home Pattern Company. III. Title: Home book of fashions, Winter 1914, Volume 1, Number 2.
  TT556.H66 1995
  646.4′07′09041—dc20   95-10181
                                             CIP

Manufactured in the United States of America
Dover Publications, Inc., 31 East 2nd Street, Mineola, N.Y. 11501

Introduction

"There are a great many ... who feel rather aghast at the prospect of future fashions, after spending a few days at a French watering place," a fashion editor commented in a 1913 year-end issue of the popular magazine, *Young Ladies' Journal.* "It is more difficult just now than I can ever remember it being to put the happy medium between 'frumpish dowdiness' and daring eccentricity." This, however, was exactly what *The Home Book of Fashions* purported to do. During a time when Paris, the source of all high fashion, was at war, this catalog "illustrated the newest," most sophisticated styles for the home sewer.

While *The Home Book of Fashions* grimly relates that "the Parisienne has no interest in the length of jackets or skirts at present [because she] has more momentous things in mind," the styles offered, unlike the fashions of most war years, revealed virtually no sign of the death of opulence—velvets, silks, brocades and laces were used freely. The only sign that the world was at war was the occasional "military effect" utilized in some trimmings and coat styles.

Unlike most pattern catalogs of the period, *The Home Book of Fashions* featured fewer severe, tailored suits, and instead, emphasized feminine, often elegant, dresses and gowns. Though the catalog was issued for the home sewer, it was also clearly for the woman who aimed to dress in the latest, most tasteful styles. While the fashions illustrated might at first glance appear to be created for the woman of wealth and leisure, headlines like "Semi-Precious Pelts," "Sensible Gifts" and "The Business Girl's Good-Sense Dress" certainly indicate that the woman who most relied on *The Home Book* was middle-class.

The Home Book of Fashions stood out from a myriad of pattern catalogs in other ways, also. Like them, it offered patterns for children's clothing and some men's items as well as women's clothing, but, more than any other pattern catalog, it was the home of sophisticated styles, even including Victorian-inspired "fancy dress," or masquerade costume patterns. Notes on the latest in accessories, millinery, fabrics and trims were sprinkled throughout the catalog generously. Articles on European design, beauty, trends and important garments that of necessity were purchased custom- or ready-made (like corsets) were also liberally included. And, foretelling the immense popularity of embroidery and other "fancy" needlework and crafts in the 'twenties, the catalog included a large number of embroidery patterns, crochet designs and craft ideas for clothing and decorative accessories.

In an age caught between the frills and furbelows of the Victorian era and the curveless, boyish look adopted in the 1920s, *The Home Book of Fashions* offered the American woman the femininity of her mother's era, while employing the more relaxed fashion freedom of the decade to come.

With an exotically draped gown, a standing ruff collar and a pointed hat punctuated with an ostrich plume, the woman of the 'teens marched her way into twentieth-century life.

KRISTINA HARRIS

[original front cover]

THE straight outlines of the popular new Basques are girlish in the extreme, particularly when worn in combination with tunic skirts, cut very short and tight as to the undergarment and full and long as to the tunic. The fronts of many of these Basques continue to form fetching sashes which tie in the back. A waist of this character is No. 8628, which is cut with long tight-fitting sleeves set into a drop-shouldered line. It has small revers, and a Robespierre collar which holds in place a lace frill. Its pattern cuts in sizes 32 to 42 inches bust measure, while No. 8629, the three-piece skirt with two-piece pointed tunics, with which it is illustrated, cuts in sizes 22 to 32 inches waist measure. In medium size you will require 3⅛ yards 36-inch silk, 3¾ yards 36-inch chiffon, 1⅝ yards 36-inch lining and ½ yard 5-inch lace. Patterns 15 cents each.

[original inside front cover]

8619-8622—Taken directly from the cartridge belts which are being so tragically employed abroad this fall, are many of the new cross-over effects shown on the new waists. The one illustrated has a distinct flavor of the Revolutionary period with its smart waistcoat. The skirt, too, is one of the most popular of the late models, for the tight underskirt contrasts sharply with the long, full tunic. This dress would make up well in a deep purple surah silk combined with velvet of a darker shade and with biscuit-colored taffeta for vests. The waist, No. 8619, cuts in sizes 32 to 44 inches bust measure, and skirt, No. 8622, in sizes 22 to 32 inches waist measure. The costume in medium size will require 5⅝ yard of 36-inch silk with 1¾ yards 36-inch contrasting velvet, 1 yard of 27-inch silk for collar and vest and 1⅛ yards 36-inch lining. Patterns 15 cents each.

Volume 1   WINTER, 1914   Number 2

THE HOME BOOK OF
FASHIONS

The Home Pattern Company, Publishers, 615 West 43d Street, New York

President, WILLIAM E. WALTER   Secretary, C. H. LUDINGTON
Treasurer, W. O. BAGLEY

Branches: Chicago, Ill. St. Louis, Mo. San Francisco, Cal. Toronto, Can.

Copyright, 1914, by The Home Pattern Company
The Words "The Ladies' Home Journal" are copyrighted and
registered as a trade-mark

THE LATEST ADVICES FROM THE RUE DE LA PAIX
FASHIONS FROM THE FRENCH CAPITAL

By ELIZABETH DRYDEN

SITTING in my hotel window and looking out onto the gardens of the Tuileries, it seems impossible to think that one is in the very theatre of war—and then a company of artillery comes down the Rue de Rivoli at a spanking gallop, or a slow-moving vehicle from the North crawls by with its load of wounded from the battle-front, and wakens one to the grim realities of conflict. Incongruous as it may seem, the thing that touches me most deeply is that I have to walk up three flights of stairs to my bedroom. The porters have all gone off to the war and I will not trust myself to the inexperienced housemaids, who would gladly run the lift for me—all of which you can read in the letters of those who are here describing the war, and so, although I am longing to tell you some of my interesting experiences, I will "knuckle down to business" and try to give you a glimpse of Paris' war-time fashions.

Had it not been for the year's terrible events, there is no question but that Paris would have had a most wonderful rue de la Paix season. We have not seen for many years so much that is absolutely new and yet both practical and wearable, and strange to say, they are still appearing in the establishments which are making the courageous effort to keep open. Some of the houses are getting up new models, making every effort to keep the "main d'oeuvre" busy—that is the great question here—how to keep the women of Paris at work. There is, of course, plenty of work for the handful of men left—and to spare.

A few days ago an American correspondent paid double rates in order to cable me: "What is the Paris preference in jacket lengths?" To her credit be it said that the Parisienne has no interest in the length of jackets or skirts at present. She has more momentous things in mind—the welfare of her father, son, or brother, the planning to make two ends meet, the eager anxiety to hear the latest news from the front, the desire to help care for the wounded and dying.

As to the designs of this or that great designer; there are at least a half dozen preferred lengths; American buyers have gone in for longer jackets, and also for those which have the long back, somewhat on the lines of a man's swallow-tail coat. Callot alone is showing the short bolero jackets. They have a delightful model in plaid taffeta and velvet, and are also showing long coats that cover almost the entire skirt, although the majority of jackets only reach just below the hips.

Cheruit's Robe-Manteau

Cheruit, who has made a great hit with her innovation the "robe-manteau," or one-piece dress, has a redingote matching the skirt beneath, which it nearly covers. This redingote is cut straight from shoulder to hem, having the new long waistline, with a fur belt and groups of pleats in the back and front. Cheruit also shows many full-skirted Russian blouses that reach to below the knee, a form that is difficult for any but a very tall figure.

Drecoll's great success is a long jacket that reaches below the knees. It is severely tailored and is very clever in cut. The slightly suggested waistline is scarcely drawn in, while the hips are closely fitted; this makes the figure very slim.

Most of Premet's jackets are of the swallow-tail form, which were launched at their advance opening in May. I think, though, that their short pointed jacket with long flaring back, finished with fur, that entirely covers the skirt, is more original and wearable, and gives a newer line to the figure.

As for skirts! They are wider in every case, but quite as varied as the jackets. Cheruit goes in for flaring godet skirts. At first they seem hard to wear, and I think that the straight line skirts, particularly those which are plaited, will be the choice of the Parisienne, when she does at last make a choice as to style.

One of the prettiest of the wider skirts is that at Premet's, which has horizontal bands formed of fine tucks passing round it at intervals. Callot clings to

narrow underskirts with full overskirts above them. A great favorite is a kilted underskirt with a pointed double overskirt, shaped like a shawl. So much for skirts.

The one-piece dress, which we are told will be worn with small furs, until the weather demands something heavier, is the season's greatest novelty. To Madame Cheruit, who gave us the "robe-manteau" a few months ago, we owe its inspiration.

Most of the one-piece dresses are almost straight in line, giving the effect of a redingote. When there is a waist it is placed very low so that it does not take away from this effect. "New" these gowns are proclaimed, and needless to say, that title is not the least asset of their success. Usually made in broadcloth, they sometimes appear in serge, velvet, or in wool velvet. Callot is showing a beauty with a full graduated tunic falling from the hips over a narrow underskirt, a handsome design in burgundy velvet is edged with mink. It has a curious redingote falling over a skirt made in a soft puff.

Callot is showing a reseda green wool velvet with an overskirt shaped like a shawl, and finished at the edges with a tiny picot, while the underskirt is made in one inch side plaits. The jacket has three flaring box plaits at each hip, with a button on the top of each.

One of the loveliest indoor models is a little satin gown by Cheruit, which has groups of side plaits in its flaring skirt. The kimono shoulders continue their line into a long, loose pointed piece that forms the back of the waist. A wonderful sash of rich plaid silk gives the gown its cachet.

The New Materials

As for materials; broadcloth is the great favorite for street wear, while velvet, the fabric par excellence for afternoon and evening wear, runs a close second. This does not mean to say that there are not a great many grosgrains, or failles, for there are; there are also a great many colored and metal brocades on fancy silk and velvet materials combined with lace, net or chiffon. There are also wool velvets of great variety much on the order of the cotton velours we had last spring. For the strictly tailored suits mostly home-spuns, serges and cheviots are used.

The colors are more subdued for daily wear, and softened and more melting for the evening. All sorts of mahogany and burgundy tones mingle with brown furs and gold embroidery and attract one by their artistic qualities as well as their newness.

Premet shows many grays and greenish tones and Cheruit show some darker blues; indeed, every one has these colors.

Worth uses royal and navy blue velvet for about everything, and for evening dresses a great deal of pink, coral, burnt orange and champagne mixed with touches of brilliant rhinestones, metal embroidery, or metal threaded lace.

I have tried to sketch for you a number of the best of the models. In the large illustration is shown one of the Redingote dresses. Of this there is a pattern, No. 8660, which you can purchase for 15 cents. It should be developed in velveteen, serge, broadcloth or taffeta with the collar, cuffs and girdle of figured silk or wide braid, or if preferred, you could make the trimmings of a contrasting shade of silk or velvet and heavily soutached. There are no patterns of the small sketches; these are merely straws thrown out to show which way the wind is blowing.

DRECOLL   PREMET   CHERUIT

CALLOT   CALLOT   DRECOLL

8660—The Redingote Dress

8631-8632 Emb. 14272   8633-8634

SUMPTUOUS AFTERNOON GOWNS OF CLOTH AND VELVET

BROADCLOTH is the fabric par excellence for winter street suits and in the dress 8631-8632, it is combined with braided white broadcloth and skunk. The braiding design No. 14272 is used on the side panels of the four-piece circular skirt, the side panels being shirred to a foundation yoke. The coat is cut in cross-over effect, and the pattern comes in sizes 32 to 42 inches bust measure while the skirt cuts in sizes 22 to 34 inches waist measure. Dress as illustrated will require in medium size 6 yards of 42-inch material with ⅜ yard 36-inch contrasting material. The braiding border is 3 inches wide and there are three yards in the pattern. Patterns 15 cents each.

8633-8634—Velvet brocade in a soft and lustrous weave is employed in developing this attractive gown. As in many of the newest models the front of the waist extends into a girdle. The only ornamentation that this elaborate fabric needs is a collar, cuffs and skirt band of lynx used with a collar of princess lace. Carved ivory buttons in graduated sizes finish the front closing of the blouse or they could be of jet or satin. The pattern is cut in sizes 32 to 44 inches bust measure and the skirt pattern comes in sizes 22 to 34 inches waist measure. The dress requires 4⅞ yards 36-inch material with ¼ yard lace for the collar. Patterns 15 cents each.

8636-8637   8640-8614 Emb. 14504

RIVALING THOSE OF CHARMEUSE AND TAFFETA

CROSS-OVER effects are still much in vogue. In the illustration, waist No. 8636 is opened over the vest of piqué while the revers and sash are of striped silk. The three-piece skirt, 8637, is cut with the front gore extending to the waistline while the side gores are gathered to a hip yoke. The pattern for the blouse cuts in sizes 34 to 44 inches bust measure and the skirt cuts in sizes 22 to 34 inches waist measure. You will require for the dress, as illus-

trated, 5⅛ yards 36-inch material, with 1⅞ yards 36-inch striped material for revers and sash and ⅞ yard 27-inch piqué for vest. Patterns 15 cents each.

8640–8614–14504—In this dress the s u r p l i c e lines of the overblouse are apparently continued by a sash of taffeta and the outlines of the blouse and bottom of skirt are braided with design No. 14504 (3 inches wide, 3 yards and 4 corners in the pattern.

Price 10 cents.). The chemisette has a wide standing collar, and turn-back cuffs finish the full-length sleeves. Blouse pattern cuts in sizes 32 to 46 inches bust measure while the skirt cuts in sizes 22 to 36 inches waist measure and you will require for the dress, as illustrated, 5⅞ yards 36-inch material, with 1 yard 27-inch taffeta for girdle and sash and ⅝ yard 36-inch contrasting material for the chemisette, collar and cuffs. Patterns 15 cents each.

THE BOLERO AND REDINGOTE DRESS FOR STREET WEAR

8638–8639

8635
Emb. 14281

A POPULAR style of fall suit is in reality a bolero waist and a skirt made of velvet and combined with fitch or opossum fur. Such a dress has a vest and collar of white satin and looks quite suitable for the street yet dressy enough for indoors. Pattern 8638 is for a waist of this character and combines well with skirt 8639, a five-gored circular model. The waist pattern comes in sizes 32 to 44 inches bust measure and the skirt pattern in sizes 22 to 36 inches waist measure. In medium size you will require 5 yards 36-inch material, with 7/8 yard 36-inch satin for collar and underpart of waist, 5 yards fur banding and 7/8 yard striped silk for girdle. Patterns 15 cents each.

8635–14281—The Redingote dress is one of the most popular models for the early winter. The blouse with its long peplum and the skirt are attached at the waistline or they can be made separately. Navy serge with trimmings of braid and soutaching from transfer pattern 14281 (3 yards in the pattern, 2 inches wide. Price 15 cents.) will give a rich effect. Pattern cuts in sizes 34 to 44 inches bust measure and will require in size 36, 5 yards 42-inch material, with 1/2 yard 36-inch satin for collar, cuffs and belt and 7/8 yard 27-inch lining for upper part of piece 7. Pattern 15 cents.

8582 8611

DAINTY DANCING FROCKS
GIRLISH FRILLS AND TUNICS

DANCING the new steps in old frocks would be like pouring new wine into old bottles, which may be why we are having so many new and fetching styles this winter. One particularly adapted to the latest dances is No. 8582. The billowy overskirt of lace supports a single rose, whose mate is perched on the shoulder of the semi-fitted Basque. Pattern cuts in sizes 34 to 42 inches bust measure, requiring in size 36, 3¾ yards 36-inch silk, 2½ yards 7-inch lace for chemisette and sleeve, 2 yards 27-inch flouncing and 1¼ yards 36-inch lining. Pattern 15 cents.

8611—The swaying of dainty flounces adds wonderfully to the grace and effectiveness of a dancing dress. Combine with these a smartly draped scarf overblouse of supple taffeta, satin or crêpe de Chine mounted on a filmy lace waist and caught with a single huge rose, and you have dress No. 8611. The pattern for this dress cuts in sizes 34 to 42 inches bust measure and you will require in size 36, 4 yards 42-inch net, 1¾ yards 30-inch silk for overblouse, 2⅜ yards 30-inch lace for underwaist, and 3½ yards lace edging for neck and sleeve frills. Pattern 15 cents.

STOUT FIGURES PRESENT AN INTERESTING PROBLEM

WHEN a woman begins to leave youthful slimness behind and sees herself growing gradually plump and then plumper, and then positively stout, life is apt to seem a tragedy. Just at present, however, fashion is kind to the stout woman, for large waists are so much the fashion that she need not lace herself in, until her discomfort shows itself in her reddened face. A dress that is in good taste for afternoon and church wear is illustrated in Nos. 8610 and 8614, which are shown in soft cashmere, trimmed with military braid. The blouse has a surplice line excellent for stout figures. The skirt is a very simple three-piece circular model and the ample width at the hem dwarfs the apparent size of the hips and bust. A motif of braiding from transfer pattern 14508 (containing six transfers of this motif and costing 10 cents) is used on the sleeve. The waist pattern cuts in sizes 34 to 44 inches bust measure and the skirt from 22 to 32 inches waist measure. For the dress in size 40 waist and 28-inch skirt you will require 5¾ yards 36-inch material, with ⅞ yard 36-inch satin for girdle and ½ yard 36-inch lace for chemisette. Patterns 15 cents each.

8609—Further to the right is illustrated another excellent model for the stout woman, a coat-dress opening in the front. Its long, simple lines are unbroken by the deep false girdle of wide basket-weave braid, and the collar and cuffs of black satin add a smart touch. The pattern cuts in sizes 34 to 46 inches bust measure, requiring in size 42, 5⅝ yards 42-inch material, with ½ yard 36-inch satin, ¾ yard 7-inch braid and 1¾ yards 36-inch lining. Pattern 15 cents.

If you will turn to page 48, you will find further suggestions as to how to deal with the stout woman's problem and other excellent styles suited to her needs.

8610–8614
Emb. 14508

8609

NOVEL BOX-PLEATED AND BLOUSED TUNICS

MANY of the new Basques and over-blouses have the effect of scarfs wrapped casually about the figure and yet into the exact cut of these garments there goes a world of thought and experience. The one illustrated at the left is mounted on a fitted foundation waist to which the sleeves are sewed. Over this is worn a loose over-waist with enlarged armscyes and long sash-ends which tie low in the back. This is worn with one of the most novel of the new skirts, a three-piece model having a tunic in the same number of gores, bloused up, giving rather the effect of Turkish trousers. The blouse pattern, No. 8600, is cut in sizes 32 to 46 inches bust measure and the skirt, No. 8603, in sizes 22 to 32 inches waist measure. Dress in medium size will require 5⅛ yards 36-inch material, with 2 yards 42-inch contrasting goods and 2¼ yards 36-inch lining. Patterns 15 cents each.

8594-8595—A simple example of the widely popular Basque is illustrated in combination with a box-pleated tunic skirt mounted on a three-piece yoke. If desired the front of the Basque could be made without fullness, being instead semi-fitted by a dart, by cutting the outside as well as the lining by section 3 of the pattern. The skirt is cut with a slightly raised waist-line and is in three-gores while the box-pleated tunic is quite straight. A dress of this style will make up well in a combination of broadcloth and messaline, or a supple taffeta. The waist pattern cuts in sizes 32 to 44 inches bust measure and the skirt pattern in sizes 22 to 32 inches waist measure. For the dress in medium size you will require 5⅜ yards 36-inch material with 1⅝ yards 36-inch contrasting silk and 2¾ yards 36-inch lining. Patterns 15 cents each.

8600-8603   8594-8595

CHARMING COSTUMES FOR WEAR AT AFTERNOON TEA
DEEP TUCKS GIVE THE THREE-TIERED EFFECT

8594-8595   8592-8577

THE combination of black and white is popular, and in this charming Basque costume, 8594-8595, it is shown to excellent advantage. Black velvet is used for the Basque deep underskirt, while the box-plaited tunic, collar and cuffs, are of white broadcloth. The fronts of the Basque are shirred under the box plait. The Basque has full-length sleeve with turn-back cuffs and a large Murat collar. Pattern for the Basque cuts in sizes 32 to 42 inches bust measure,

the skirt in sizes 22 to 42 inches waist measure. Dress requires, as illustrated, 2¼ yards of 54-inch broadcloth, with 2⅞ yards of 36-inch velvet, and 2¾ yards of 30-inch lining. Price 15 cents each.

8592-8577—Plaid and plain taffetas are combined in this attractive Basque dress. The fronts of Basque are cut to form a sash. It has full-length sleeves, turn-back cuffs, and a Directoire collar. The skirt is

one of the newest two-piece models, measuring in size 24, 2⅛ yards at lower edge, and has two deep tucks and a hem. The pattern of the Basque cuts in sizes 32 to 42 inches bust measure, and the skirt in sizes 22 to 32 inches waist measure. Dress, as illustrated, requires in size 36, 4¼ yards of 36-inch plaid material, and 2⅞ yards 36-inch plain material, with ½ yard 36-inch material for collar and cuffs. Patterns 15 cents each.

UP-TO-DATE AND BECOMING FURS
POPULAR SEMI-PRECIOUS PELTS

SAMSON & HUBBARD
BOSTON

SAMSON & HUBBARD
BOSTON

CHINCHILLA combined artistically with skunk in a square muff and a small throw scarf that would become almost any woman.

ERMINE, with its cold beauty, should only be worn by the woman with warm coloring and is at its best in the evening.

THE tunic line, so much the vogue in dresses, is reproduced in the newest fur coats, as in this garment of French seal and smoked fox.

REVILLON
FRERES

SAMSON & HUBBARD
BOSTON

CHINCHILLA squirrel, with its wonderful blending of shades, is almost as handsome as the expensive chinchilla and wears better.

THE delicate yellow and brown coloring of fitch blends well with the popular French sealskin and makes an inexpensive but sumptuous looking set. (At the right.)

A HANDSOME skunk set will wear a lifetime with good care. The one above has a straight throw scarf and an attractive novelty muff.

LEOPARD skin and cub bear are used together in the novel set at the left, which would be found particularly becoming to a youthful wearer.

FASCINATING FROCKS IN DRAMATIC OFFERINGS

By ELEANOR RAEBURN

PAULINE FREDERICK
in "Innocent"

FASHION returns to the stage, this early season, with all the charm of former days, when Paris was *not* a minus quantity. Most of the current plays show admirable costumes from the American sources, but Pauline Frederick wearing Drécoll effects in "Innocent" is a striking exception. Her gowns comprise a Manchu costume of ciel-blue crêpe—in glorified pajama style, with self-colored embroidery; a dinner toilette of silver-embroidered chiffon over white satin (illustrated); two négligées—one a Bendel tea-gown of white satin, with appliqué-lace shoulder drapery; a stunning afternoon frock of turquoise taffeta, overhung with three lapping gold lace flounces, worn with a Moyen-Age coat of turquoise satin; and an evening toilette of beaded emerald tulle over white charmeuse.

The gowns in "Under Cover" have won a renown commensurate with the success of that play; notably an evening costume worn by Lily Cahill (Illustration 4) made of white charmeuse, bordered on the Greek tunic and bodice with mother-of-pearl banding that matches the pointed girdle. Lucile Watson also displays smart toilettes, particularly an evening gown of black jetted net and satin, with a flesh-tinted corsage. In "Twin Beds" Madge Kennedy appears in a dainty dancing frock of white crystal-embroidered tulle, deep tabs forming the tunic, with a pale-blue folded sash. Ray Cox exploits a trained toilette of burnt orange charmeuse.

"On Trial," another of the current successes, discloses two striking gowns; that, for evening, worn by Helene Lackaye, combining gold-embossed turquoise chiffon with a bodice of cyclamen pink chiffon; and Mary Ryan's afternoon gown of gray crêpe de Chine, having a full plaited tunic that falls from a wide folded sash of the crêpe and black velvet, in front; the back drapery descending from the shoulders.

John Drew's play, which usually sets the Autumn pace in styles, is disappointing in "The Prodigal Husband"; only the "sweet simplicity" frock of Jessie Glendenning—made of white marquisette and satin—and the dinner costume of Grace Carlyle—combining steel-blue chiffon tunics over white satin, with a relief of gold-and-blue brocade—meriting attention. In "The Girl from Utah," Julia Sanderson wears very simple, but lovely, frocks—one, of white chiffon and black satin, with black monkey fur (Illustration 5).

Margaret Illington, on tour, has acquired stunning costumes for "Within the Law." Frances Starr returns to repeat her toilette successes of last year in "The Secret"—the illustrated one of white charmeuse and unspotted ermine being a favorite. Janet Beecher's smart frocks in "The Vanishing Bride" included the pictured one of black charmeuse. A girlish dancing frock worn by Marilynn Miller in "The Passing Show of 1914," made of accordion-plaited blond lace, gathered to a wide ceinture, has black velvet shoulder bands. In "The Elder Son" Cynthia Brooke wears exceptionally good clothes, particularly one gown of tête-de-nègre taffeta.

MARGARET ILLINGTON
in "Within the Law"

MARILYNN MILLER
in "The Passing Show of 1914"

FRANCES STARR as She Appears in "The Secret"

JANET BEECHER
in "The Vanishing Bride"

1.—BERNICE BUCK, now on tour in "A Pair of Sixes," in a walking costume of midnight blue gabardine, combined with self-colored satin.

2.—HAZEL DAWN, appearing this season in "The Debutante," shown in a white charmeuse and ninon dancing frock, with gold-embroidered ceinture and bodice.

3.—JOBYNA HOWLAND, in "The Third Party," exploits a chic costume of white d'Alençon lace over turquoise taffeta. Lace Medici and taffeta sash.

4.—LILY CAHILL, in "Under Cover," reveals costume novelty in a flesh-tinted white charmeuse evening gown. Greek tunic, with mother-of-pearl girdle and banding.

5.—JULIA SANDERSON, now playing in "The Girl from Utah," wears a dancing frock of white chiffon, black satin, and black monkey fur.

6.—LOUISE DREW, seen in "It Pays to Advertise," displays a kilt-plaited tunic costume of white charmeuse, with a black panne Spencer waist.

SASH WAISTS AND BLOUSED UP SKIRTS ARE NEW

8600–8603—So popular has the Basque become that waists of all sorts and conditions have sashes e x t e n d i n g below the waistline, some tying in the front and others in the back. One of the latter is illustrated here in combination with skirt 8603 which embodies a novel idea, in that the tunic is bloused up onto the drop-skirt, a feature which appears on many of the imported models. The pattern for the waist cuts in sizes 32 to 46 inches bust measure and the skirt in sizes 22 to 32 inches waist measure. For the dress in medium size you will require 6⅜ yards 36-inch silk with 1¾ yards 36-inch contrasting material for underwaist, ½ yard 42-inch net for collar and 2¼ yards 36-inch lining. Patterns 15 cents each.

8590–8591—Velvet and satin are much used in combination this season, frequently being of the same color, though the richness of the two fabrics is apt to be more apparent if the velvet is a shade or two darker than the satin. Many of the new waists have deep corselet girdles like 8590 and these are usually worn with full gathered skirts that have two or more bands of trimming near the hem, which is often heavily weighted with shot. The pattern for the waist cuts in sizes 32 to 44 inches bust measure and for the straight gathered skirt in sizes 22 to 32 inches waist measure. In medium size you will require for the dress 4¼ yards 36-inch silk with 1⅛ yards 36-inch velvet for the corselet and trimming bands. Patterns 15 cents each.

8600–8603   8590–8591

MILITARY EFFECTS IN BOTH LONG AND SHORT COATS

8561

8615—8618

8561—This serviceable coat is cut on the most approved lines and would be found becoming to many different types. Cheviot, serge and broadcloth are appropriate materials to use and if the collar, revers and cuffs are cut from velvet, it would serve for dressy afternoon wear. The pattern cuts in sizes 34 to 44 inches bust measure and contains a double coachman's cape which may be used to give extra warmth as well as a smart appearance. Size 36 requires 4¾ yards 42-inch material with ½ yard 18-inch velvet for collar and cuffs. Price 15 cents.

8615—8618—The influence of the European war is giving the dress designers many inspirations and here is shown one of the best interpretations of this type of coat. It is worn with a six-gored skirt having groups of three plaits at each seam and a hip yoke and pockets which may be omitted if desired. The skirts are now worn short, some being five inches from the floor. The coat is quite elaborately trimmed with military braid and the Directoire collar is of astrakhan, which fur, as well as its many imitations, is being used to a large extent on the newest models. The pattern cuts in sizes 32 to 44 inches bust measure and the pattern for the skirt cuts in sizes 22 to 32 inches waist measure. You will require for the suit as illustrated, 7⅜ yards 36-inch broadcloth, and 12 yards of braid for trimming. Price of patterns 15 cents each.

8436

8570

8424

WINTER COATS OF SHAGGY TWEEDS AND CHEVIOTS

FOR solid comfort in really cold weather there is nothing more sensible and at the same time good looking than the Inverness coat. To be true to the original, it should be made sleeveless with an enlarged armscye, but as many prefer sleeves, they are included in pattern No. 8436, which may be made in either of two lengths. The pattern cuts in sizes 32, 36, 40 and 44 inches bust measure, size 36 requiring 5⅜ yards 42-inch material. Pattern 15 cents.

8570—Simple, conservative good style is shown in pattern No. 8570 which may be made up in the length illustrated with shawl collar, or if preferred in ⅞ length with standing collar and a deep crushed belt with pockets. Made of a shaggy tweed with the collar and cuffs of marmot or caracul fur, this would be ideal for cold weather. The pattern cuts in sizes 32 to 46 inches bust measure, size 36 requiring 2¾ yards 54-inch material. Pattern 15 cents.

8424—The roomy comfort of the Balmacaan coat is well appreciated. The one illustrated has a novelty in cut, in that the body portion is in one piece without underarm seam. For hard wear, this could be developed in black and white cheviot with the collar and cuffs of fur fabric. The pattern cuts in sizes 32, 36, 40 and 44 inches bust measure, size 36 requiring 3⅞ yards 54-inch material with ⅜ yard 36-inch contrasting material for collar and cuffs. Pattern 15 cents.

BOTH CHIC AND BEAUTY IN WINTER HATS

IT IS on Fifth Avenue that, even in early Fall, one is able to discern with considerable certainty just what the modes of the winter will be. With reference to hats, in sketch 1 is shown a toque of velvet from Knox, perhaps a bit severe, with a trimming of moiré ribbon and a flat, pleated pompon, which is quite unmistakably for wear on the morning shopping tour. And following this one sees a girlish, three-cornered sailor of black velvet with protruding tufts of coq feathers, pictured in sketch 2. For morning wear this, but of a sufficient dressiness to look entirely in place at the luncheon or even the tea-table. And then a sailor, sketched in No. 3, which entirely refuses the simplicity which usually marks the sailor hat. Its lines are straight and its trimming audacious, consisting only of a made quill of self-material, but to be worn at all, Rosenblum, the maker, insists that it must be worn with a rakish tilt. Much like this in trimming but differing wholly in shape is the toque from Greenhut, in sketch No. 4, reminding one of a triangle to what a height does it ascend on one side and to what a mere nothing it descends on the other.

Following this variety for the maid, surely the matron cannot be overlooked, and a glance around discovers a so-called toque of velvet with a soft crown almost lost to sight between the high front and higher back of the upstanding brim, which brim, by the way, Rosenblum has encircled by silver tinsel swallows with outspread wings and tails. Sketch No. 5.

And then, the distinctly dressy hats, made to be beautiful first and useful, perhaps. A notable example has been sketched in figure

No. 6, consisting of a crown of velvet, a halo effect of net, black or white or gold, and a touch of brilliance in the huge flower which clings lightly to the brim. Another type of the graceful hat is sketched in figure No. 7, a broad-brimmed sailor of heavy silk velvet, flaunting aloft like a lone pine tree, a very tall feather of uncurled ostrich. The beauty of these two fabrics alone would make any hat beautiful, and to this Knox has added grace of line. But not to be overlooked is a hat by Rosenblum distinctly for the very young girl or debutante with sloping brim and low, round crown of silk beaver. A wealth of fitch fur surrounds the crown and, massed at one side, weighs down the already drooping brim. Sketch No. 8.

8630-8573

8593
Emb. 14284

8615-8464

8630-8573   8593   8615-8464

CHIC SIMPLICITY IN

8630-8573—This simple front-closing Basque has a novel back which gives the appearance of being cut in one with the front and extending into a sash. It has full-length flaring sleeves and a large turn-down collar. The three-gored skirt shown with this Basque has a three-piece gathered tunic. The Basque pattern cuts for ladies and misses in sizes 34 to 42 inches bust measure, while the skirt cuts for misses only in sizes 16, 17 and 18 and you will require for the dress in size 36 bust, 6⅜ yards 36-inch material. Price 15 cents each.

8593-14284—Many of the newest serge dresses are elaborately trimmed with soutache or rat-tail braiding. In the illustration is shown an especially attractive one with three rows of braiding done in rat-tail on girdle and bottom of tunic. The pattern cuts in sizes 16, 17 and 18,

WINTER COSTUMES

requiring in size 18, 4½ yards 42-inch material. Price 15 cents. Design No. 14284 is 2½ inches wide and 3 yards are included in the pattern. Price 10 cents.

8615-8464—Although copied directly from her brother's military coat, this garment retains plenty of femininity. It has two styles of collar and full-length sleeves and cuts in sizes 32 to 44 inches bust measure. It is worn with tunic skirt, No. 8464, which is a two-piece model with raised waistline and with or without long tunic and deep belt. Developed in navy blue gabardine, with braidings of black and buttons of brass, this costume would be especially attractive. The skirt cuts in sizes 16, 17 and 18 and you will require for the suit as illustrated, 5⅜ yards 42-inch material, with 3¼ yards of braid and 9 yards of cord. Price 15 cents each.

ACCESSORIES TO THE WINTER TOILETTE

BEADS of jet or steel are used on many of the new velvet hand-bags while some are made of porcelain or glass beads in conventional or floral design.

WAISTCOATS of lace and dimity have high rolling collars and revers of hand embroidery and are used with either strictly tailored, or semi-tailored suits.

PENDANTS of jet and rhinestones are hung on narrow silk cords and finished with long and heavy silk tassels.

ROMAN striped ribbon in soft colorings are used for many of the new handbags which are often novel in shape.

THE new mesh bags are fitted with convenient silver toilet articles, each fitting into its own particular pocket. Linings are of chamois.

HEAVY cotton webbing forms the belt shown above. The buckle is covered with the same material. Beneath is shown a girdle of white suede with trimmings of patent leather, a smart combination.

SHOWN above is a becoming collar of embroidered net, plain in front and plaited in the back. The edges are hemstitched.

DAINTY hemstitched folds of lawn trim the dimity collar shown above, while the one beneath, which is a combination of waistcoat, girdle, sailor collar and chemisette is of moiré and an embroidered batiste.

A HEAVILY corded ribbon in a Roman stripe design is the material used for the deep girdle-belt illustrated above.

THE smart fan above is made of filigree celluloid in black and white, but it also can be had in other combinations.

BLACK chiffon, spangled with almost invisible sequins is the material of which the lace trimmed fan above is made. The sticks are jet.

THE BUSINESS GIRL'S GOOD-SENSE DRESS

8379-8568

8567-8577

8579

8379
8568

8567
8577

8579

8379-8568—A smart mannish shirtwaist, such as all business women should wear, is shown in combination with one of the long tunic skirts. The pattern for the shirtwaist includes two styles of sleeves and collar and also a pocket which can be omitted if desired, while the skirt pattern cuts in three gores as does the tunic. Waist pattern No. 8379 cuts in sizes 32 to 48 inches bust measure, requiring in size 36, 3⅛ yards 30-inch material. The skirt pattern cuts in sizes 22 to 32 inches waist measure, requiring in size 24, 3¼ yards 42-inch material with 1⅞ yards 36-inch lining. Patterns 15 cents each.

8567-8577—Flowered taffetas, crêpe de Chine and satins all wear well enough to deserve a place in the business girl's wardrobe. They are suitable for the charming new waists with deep French yokes and tight sleeves which combine so well with the skirts whose deep tucks give the effect of tunics. Pattern No. 8567 is for a waist of this character and the skirt is No. 8577. The former cuts in sizes 32 to 42 inches bust measure and the skirt in sizes 22 to 32 inches waist measure. In medium sizes you will require 9⅝ yards 30-inch silk. Patterns 15 cents each.

8579—For business or house-work, a dress that is practical and becoming is No. 8579. The blouse is in surplice style, while the skirt is in three gores with a four-piece tunic. The pattern cuts in sizes 34 to 46 inches bust measure, requiring in size 36, 6⅛ yards 36-inch material with ½ yard 24-inch contrasting goods and 1½ yards 36-inch lining. Pattern 15 cents.

SMART STREET SUITS FOR THE DEBUTANTE

8533–8549

8615–8618

8627

8533
8549

8615
8618

8627

8533–8549—Blue serge combined with Roman striped taffeta is used in making this attractive suit, which will appeal equally to the young girl and the matron. The pattern for the coat comes for ladies and misses in sizes 32 to 44 inches bust measure, while the skirt comes in sizes 22 to 32 inches waist measure. As illustrated the suit will require 7½ yards 36-inch material, with 1¼ yards 36-inch material for collar, cuffs and cape lining. Patterns 15 cents each.

8615–8618—Military effects are always smart, especially on the young girl and in this illustration the simplest form is shown. The coat has two styles of collar and full-length sleeves. The pattern cuts in sizes 32 to 44 inches bust measure, and the skirt—which is a six-gored model, closing at the left side—comes in sizes 22 to 34 inches waist measure, and it may be made with or without the yoke and pocket facings. As illustrated, the suit will require 7⅜ yards 36-inch material, with 3¼ yards of braid. Price of patterns 15 cents each.

8627—A decidedly military coat effect is given in this one-piece tunic dress. It consists of a semi-fitted double-breasted Basque, with standing collar and full-length sleeves with turn-back cuffs, lengthened by a three-piece skirt and tunic with revers that may be turned back and buttoned to the back of the coat. The pattern comes in sizes 34 to 42 inches bust measure and will require in size 36, 2⅞ yards 42-inch material, with 2¼ yards 36-inch contrasting material for skirt, collar and cuffs. Price of pattern 15 cents.

GIRLS' NEW HOLIDAY CLOTHES

8533-14063—Ladies' and Misses' single-breasted coat to be made with turn-down collar or with shawl collar. Two styles of capes are given in the pattern and the one illustrated hangs in the back only. Cuts in sizes 32 to 44 inches bust measure requiring in size 36, 3¼ yards 42-inch material. Pattern 15 cents. Pattern No. 14063 contains several different styles of frogs. Price 10 cents.

7942—Misses' three-piece skirt with slightly raised waistline closing in the front, the back fullness arranged in gathers or tucks and to be made with or without shaped belt and pockets. In this case, it is made of gray broadcloth and the pockets are omitted. The pattern cuts in three sizes, 16, 17 and 18, size 18 requiring 2⅞ yards 42-inch material. The price of pattern 15 cents.

8578

8571

8533
7942
Emb. 14063

8436

8533-7942   8436   8578   8571

8436—Inverness coats are very popular for the young girl. This one is cut full length and perforated for shorter length and may be cut with or without set-in sleeves and with square or round corners on the bottom of coat and cape. Pattern cuts for ladies and misses in sizes 32 to 44 inches bust measure. Size 36 requires 6½ yards of 42-inch material. Price of pattern 15 cents.

8578—A blue serge dress with the underskirt facing of blue striped serge and collar, cuffs and belt of white linen is shown. The blouse opens in front and has full length sleeves, perforated for shorter length. The three-piece skirt has a three-piece tunic. Size 18 requires 4 yards of 42-inch material with ⅝ yard 36-inch striped material for underskirt and 1⅝ yards 27-inch lining. Price of pattern 15 cents.

8571—Misses' Basque dress with Medici collar or small sailor collar, full-length sleeves with deep cuffs and a three-piece skirt with straight-plaited tunic. This would be attractive developed in crêpe de Chine, charmeuse or broadcloth. Cuts in sizes 14, 16, 17 and 18 years, size 16 requires 4½ yards of 42-inch material with 1⅛ yards 36-inch contrasting material and 1 yard 36-inch lining. Price 15 cents.

DRESSY FROCKS FOR FESTIVE WINTER EVENINGS

8463
8573

8584

8630
8464

8463
8573

8584

8630
8464

8463-8573—This charming combination of plain and flowered taffeta would make an excellent dress for the young girl for informal evening wear. The raglan waist is cut for ladies and misses in sizes 34 to 42 inches bust measure and the full-length sleeves are perforated for shorter length and the front of the waist may be worn turned back over the vest of chiffon. The skirt is cut in sizes 16, 17 and 18 years. Dress as illustrated requires in size 36, 3 yards 36-inch silk for tunic and 2⅞ yards 36-inch contrasting material for waist and underskirt facing, with 1⅞ yards 30-inch lining. Price of patterns 15 cents each.

8584—The new laces are so sheer as to closely resemble a cob-web and for this reason they are well adapted to the many flounced dresses like the picture above. A taffeta girdle and chiffon flowers at the waist and on the skirt give the touch of color needed. Pattern cuts in three sizes,

16, 17 and 18 years and you will require for size 18, 11¼ yards of 11-inch ruffling, 7¾ yards 7-inch ruffling, and ¾ yard 27-inch silk and ⅜ yard 36-inch lining. Price of pattern 15 cents.

8630-8464—The combination of plain and checked taffetas is shown to great advantage in this dress which consists of a ladies' and misses' Basque waist and a two-gored skirt having a two-piece over-skirt. The front of the Basque extends into a sash in the back and it opens in the front while the skirt has a flaring tunic of the plaid taffeta. Basque cuts in sizes 34 to 42 inches bust measure and in size 36 requires 2⅞ yards of 36-inch material with ⅛ yard embroidery for the shield. The skirt cuts in sizes 16, 17 and 18 years, size 18 requires 2 yards 36-inch material for the tunic and 2½ yards of 36-inch material for underskirt. Price 15 cents each.

APRONS ARE SENSIBLE GIFTS
NEW BUNGALOW COVER-ALLS

7311

7311   Emb. 14528

8626

8123
Emb. 14191

8249

7307

8019

8626

7307—An attractive gift for the housewife or her maid servant is an apron made from pattern 7307, made in any one of three styles. The pattern cuts in one size and will require in the style illustrated, 3½ yards 27-inch material. 15 cents.

7311-14528—Two illustrations of this pattern are shown, though it includes four possibilities. The embroidered initial is from No. 14528 which contains 375 transfers of one initial. 15 cents. Apron pattern cuts in one size; full material requirements on pattern envelope. Pattern 15 cents.

8019—Probably the simplest apron to make is 8019, which would be charming in tan or blue chambray. Cuts in sizes 32, 36 and 40 inches bust measure, requiring for size 36, 4⅜ yards of 27-inch material, with ½ yard 22-inch contrasting goods. Pattern 10 cents.

8123-14191—Develop this a p r o n in plaid gingham and embroider a spray of holly (transfer pattern 14191. Price 10 cents.) and you will have an attractive gift. Cuts in sizes 32, 36, 44 and 48 inches bust measure, requiring in size 36, 5⅜ yards 27-inch material. Pattern 10 cents.

8249—Absolutely staple in design is apron 8249. It is one of the most comfortable and practical aprons and pattern includes a sweeping cap and sleeve protectors. Cuts in sizes 32, 36, 40

and 44 inches bust measure, requiring in size 36, 5¾ yards 27-inch material. Pattern 15 cents.

8626—Included in this apron pattern are seven sections which can be combined in a variety of ways, two being illustrated on this page. Pattern cuts in one size and costs 15 cents. Full directions and material requirements on envelope.

7307   8019   8123   8249

MILITARY STYLES MAKE BRAIDS POPULAR

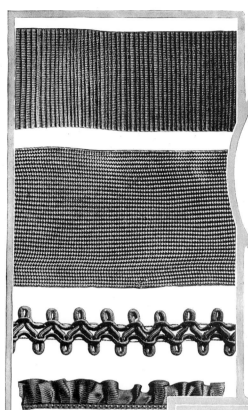

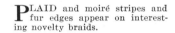

LARGE ornaments of braid, copied from those worn by army officers, decorate many of the new winter suits.

PLAITED and frilled braids are attractive novelties, while basket-weaves and gimp are good.

PLAID and moiré stripes and fur edges appear on interesting novelty braids.

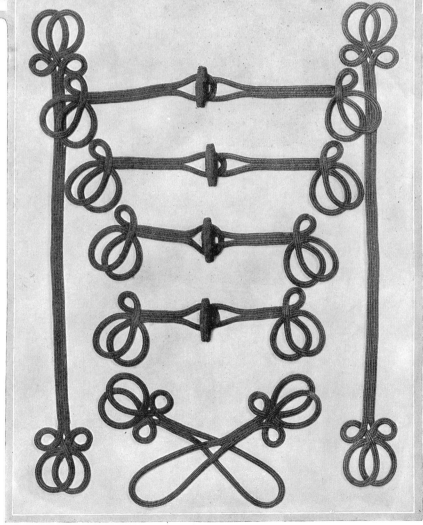

MANY of the new frogs fasten much like hooks-and-eyes with tongues that fold back.

THE fact that our minds are constantly filled with thoughts of war has made it natural that there should be a great revival of military styles. This being the case the softer and more feminine forms of embroidery have disappeared and the sterner type of military braiding is used instead. Heavy basket-weave braids are often 10 inches in width, while the variety of frogs and other braid ornaments is positively bewildering. Not content to put out plain braids, the manufacturers frequently weave them in striped effects, using the plain basket-weave alternately with rough woven plaids or printed moiré stripes. Some of the braids are edged with tiny ball fringe, while others have thin strips of fitch or coney fur.

ON MANY severely tailored suits there appear elaborate braid decorations on the order of the set illustrated above, which includes a graduated set of four frogs, two long ornaments for the sleeves and two shorter ones for epaulets, all in handsome black silk braid.

SHOWN above is the good example of the small braid tassel and below it one of the new frogs, which after slipping through the loop buttons back upon itself, giving a fastening at once firm and handsome.

GIFTS YOU CAN PURCHASE OR MAKE AT HOME

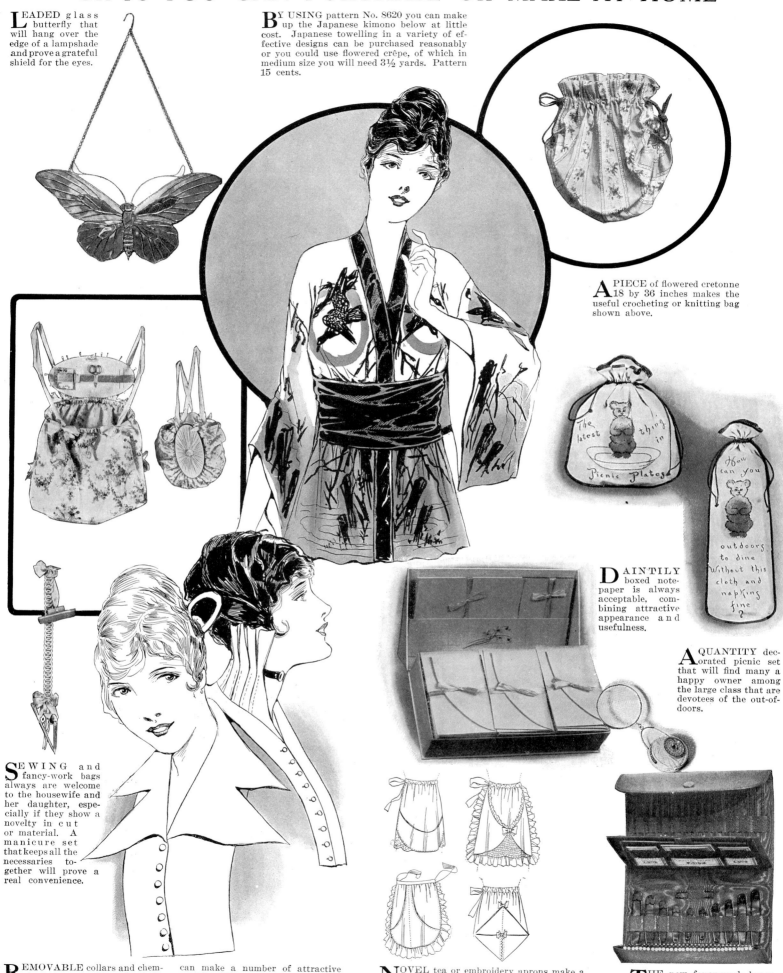

LEADED glass butterfly that will hang over the edge of a lampshade and prove a grateful shield for the eyes.

BY USING pattern No. 8620 you can make up the Japanese kimono below at little cost. Japanese towelling in a variety of effective designs can be purchased reasonably or you could use flowered crêpe, of which in medium size you will need 3½ yards. Pattern 15 cents.

A PIECE of flowered cretonne 18 by 36 inches makes the useful crocheting or knitting bag shown above.

DAINTILY boxed note-paper is always acceptable, combining attractive appearance and usefulness.

A QUANTITY decorated picnic set that will find many a happy owner among the large class that are devotees of the out-of-doors.

SEWING and fancy-work bags always are welcome to the housewife and her daughter, especially if they show a novelty in cut or material. A manicure set that keeps all the necessaries together will prove a real convenience.

REMOVABLE collars and chemisettes are in favor for holiday gifts and by purchasing pattern No. 8607 and a few lengths of piqué, lawn, dimity, or batiste you can make a number of attractive models. The pattern envelope will give you many good ideas and tell you just how much material to buy. The pattern is 10 cents.

NOVEL tea or embroidery aprons make a most acceptable gift. You may purchase a pattern (No. 8626) for these which contains seven pieces to be used in various combinations and costs 15 cents.

THE new fancy-work bracelet holds the crochet cotton or silk and a leather case carries a complete sewing outfit in a neat and compact shape.

COMFORTABLE WINTER CLOTHES FOR DOLLS

8596

8597

8596

8597

8012

8012

8597

8009

8055

7357

8596

BOY doll set, 7357. A single-breasted peasant coat with round collar, a cap, two Russian blouse suits, in peasant style. Sizes 14, 18, 22 and 26, size 18 requires for the coat 1 yard 24-inch material, with ¼ yard 18-inch contrasting material. Price 15 cents.

8009—Girl doll set. Gathered dress that may hang loose or be shirred in at low waist-line, princess slip and underwaist closing at back. For the dress any sizes requires ⅞ yard 27-inch material with ¼ yard 18-inch embroidery. Cuts in sizes 14, 18 and 22. Price 10 cents.

8012—Girl doll set. A coat, a Russian blouse suit, a coat suit, consisting of a two-piece skirt and coat with vest and Robespierre collar, a Tamo'-shanter hat and a sectional hat. Cuts in sizes 14, 18 and 22. Material requirements to be found on the pattern envelope. Price 10 cents.

8055—Baby doll set, including a coat, a cap, peasant dress, sacque, wrapper, nightgown, petticoat, tucked petticoat with waist, and a shirt. Cuts in sizes 14, 18 and 22. For the coat and cap, you will require 2⅛ yards 27-inch material and 1 yard ribbon. Price 15 cents.

8596—Girl doll set, consisting of a single-breasted cape-coat, automobile hood, three dresses, a petticoat and a combination. Cuts in 3 sizes, 14, 18 and 22. Material requirements of each article will be found on the pattern envelope. Price 15 cents.

8597—Boy doll set, consisting of an Oliver Twist suit, a sailor suit, a balmacaan coat, a romper and a union suit and two styles of hats. Cuts in sizes 14, 18 and 22. Two suits are illustrated here. Material requirements will be found on envelope. Price 15 cents.

WINTER CLOTHES FOR THE LITTLE FOLKS

DRESSES of this type, 8446, can have several white linen waists to go with the one skirt. Comes in sizes 2 to 12 years. Size 8 requires 1¾ yards 36-inch material, with 1 yard 36-inch material for waist. Pattern 15 cents.

8457—Tweed would make up very satisfactorily in this rough-and-ready single-breasted raglan coat. Comes in sizes 4 to 14 years, size 10 requiring 2⅝ yards 42-inch material, with ½-yard 27-inch contrasting goods for trimming sections. Pattern 15 cents.

8491—Appropriate for all-round wear is this dress in long-waisted style, to be worn with straight trousers or knickerbockers. Cuts in sizes 1 to 4 years. Size 2 requires 2¼ yards 36-inch material, with ⅜-yard 36-inch contrasting goods. Price 15 cents.

8544—Cream net frills upon pink silk make this party frock as dainty as can be desired. Comes in sizes 8 to 14 years, size 12 requiring 3½ yards 27-inch goods and 2 yards 42-inch net. Price 15 cents.

8564—Most becoming are the lines of this overblouse dress, trimmed with embroidery design No. 14481. (Price 10 cents.) Cuts in sizes 6 to 12 years. Size 10 requires 2¾ yards 36-inch material, 1⅜ yards 36-inch goods and 3¼ yards edging for guimpe. Pattern 15 cents.

8583—Broadcloth is just the thing for this long-waisted coat with side or box-plaited skirt. Cuts in sizes 4 to 10 years, size 8 requiring 2½ yards 42-inch goods, with ⅜-yard 36-inch contrasting material. Price 15 cents.

8585—Gray serge, with black satin collar, cuffs and buttons is used for this raglan coat with circular skirt section. Comes in sizes 4 to 14 years, size 10 requiring 2¾ yards 42-inch material, with ⅜-yard 27-inch contrasting goods. Price 15 cents.

8608—Russian blouse suits of white serge, are very popular for dressier wear. Comes in sizes 2 to 6 years, size 4 requiring 3⅛ yards 36-inch material and ½-yard 36-inch contrasting goods. Pattern 15 cents.

8585

8564
Emb. 14481

8585   8457   8583 8608   8491   8544   8446   8564

8457   8491   8583   8608   8544   8446

FOR INDOORS OR OUT

ONE attractive way of making up this Oliver Twist suit, 8142, is to use gray linen for the straight trousers, collar and cuffs and white batiste for the shirtwaist, which has applied box-plaits. Cuts in sizes 4 to 10 years, size 8 requiring 1¼ yards 36-inch linen and 1¾ yards 36-inch batiste. Price 15 cents.

8476—The little man who wears this double-breasted overcoat, having small round collar and patch pockets, will feel quite grown-up, for is this not a duplicate of his big brother's coat? Comes in sizes 2 to 14 years, size 8 requiring 2½ yards 42-inch material and ¼ yard 18-inch silk for collar. Price 15 cents.

8481—Just the thing for cool and also stormy w e a t h e r is this c o a t of double-faced material, a s t h e circular cape may be made removable when the coat itself is sufficient protection. Comes in sizes 2 to 14 years. Size 8 requires 2⅞ yards 42-inch double-faced material. Price 15 cents.

8576—Wise mothers who must dress a few tots, select one-piece dresses which slip on over the head, made of blue serge with patent leather belt. Cuts in sizes

2 to 10 years, size 6 requiring 2⅛ yards 36-inch material and ¼ yard 12-inch goods for collar. Price 15 cents.

8585—Long-waisted dresses a r e always becoming to l i t t l e girls. This model has a box-plaited skirt of brown repp, buttoning to a waist of tan linen. Cuts in sizes 4 to 10 years, size 8 requiring 1⅞ yards 36-inch material for waist and 2 yards 36-inch goods for skirt, belt, collar and cuffs. Price 15 cents.

8599—Sailing in the wake of her elder sister's style, the younger one has also adopted the Basque in lines becoming to her figure, trimming it with black braid. Cuts in sizes 6 to 14 years. Size 10 requires 2¾ yards 36-inch material, ⅝ yard 36-inch contrasting goods and 7¾ yards of braid. Pattern 15 cents.

8606—Another very pretty Basque dress is this model, which even has a three-piece tunic. The dress opens in front, has a two-piece skirt, full-length sleeve, with turn-back cuff and sailor collar. Comes in sizes 6 to 14 years. Size 10 requires 3⅛ yards 36-inch material and ⅜ yard 30-inch contrasting goods. Price 15 cents.

8142   8476   8576   8585   8606   8481

8599   8142   8599   8476   8576   8585   8606   8481   8481

SUGGESTIONS FOR THE FANCY DRESS BALL

5959

8078

7461   7461   6409

7083

7298

6407

5959—What small boy doesn't like to picture himself as a blood-thirsty and savage Indian chief, armed with a tomahawk and scalping knife, ready to strike terror into the breast of more peaceful people? The pattern of such a costume cuts in sizes 4 to 12 years, requiring in size 8, 2½ yards 36-inch goods, and 6½ yards of fringe. Pattern 15 cents.

7461—A pattern that has possibility for several developments is No. 7461, as it can either be a shepherdess or Martha Washington, or you can make up the garment with a full gathered skirt, stiffening the hem to make it stand out. Then with a bodice of black velvet and double frills of lace at sleeve and throat, you can be a French Marquise. The pattern cuts in sizes 32 to 44 inches bust measure and on the pattern envelope you will find full material requirements. Pattern 15 cents.

6409—Men usually "feel foolish" in costume but they are most comfortable in a Colonial or Directoire costume, which, by lengthening the trousers and wearing a high white hat, could be an Uncle Sam suit. The pattern cuts in sizes 24 to 44 inches breast measure, requiring in size 36, 4 yards 24-inch figured material 3¼ yards plain goods and ½ yard of 36-inch lawn. Pattern 15 cents.

7083—To a girl with brilliant coloring nothing is more becoming than the demure Quakeress costume, No. 7083. The pattern includes a cap, cuffs, double fichu and apron. The pattern cuts in sizes 34 to 44 inches bust measure and will require in any size 3¼ yards 36-inch material with 2 yards of ribbon for the cap. Pattern 15 cents.

7298—What would a fancy dress dance be without its quota of clowns? The pattern for a clown's costume is No. 7298 and can be worn by ladies, misses, men or boys, as it cuts in sizes 26, 30, 34, 38 and 40 inches bust or breast measure and is so voluminous as to be suited to any figure. It will require in size 34, 8½ yards 36-inch material. Pattern 15 cents.

8078—To many people in whom the spirit of their Puritan ancestors is strong, a domino is the only suitable costume for the fancy dress ball. In its enveloping folds one can enter into mad revels, with all the abandon that entire concealment of one's person permits. Made of satin, cashmere, or percale, according to one's pocket-book, this will add the touch of strong simple color that will set off the more elaborate costumes. The pattern cuts in sizes 32, 36, 40 and 44 inches bust or breast measure and will require in size 36, 9⅝ yards 36-inch material. Price 15 cents.

6407—There is something so bewitching about a witch that sooner or later every woman has to appear in a witch's costume, and a charming one is found in pattern No. 6407, which includes the vicious looking cats that appear on the cap and on the hem of the skirt. A costume of this kind should be developed in midnight black or firey red material and a broom should be carried, so that the fascinating lady can fly away at a moment's notice. Pattern cuts in sizes 32 to 44 inches bust measure and you will find complete material requirements on the pattern envelope. Pattern 15 cents.

8078   7461   7461   6409   7083   7298   6407

SMART TOUCHES FOR WINTER GARMENTS

8463—Ladies' and Misses' raglan waist with gathered fronts, flaring collar, vest and full-length sleeves perforated for shorter length. Cuts in sizes 34 to 42 inches bust measure. Size 36 requires 2½ yards 36-inch material. Price 15 cents.

8465—Misses' long waisted dress closing at the back, V neck, small collar, and full-length sleeves perforated for shorter length. Cuts in sizes 14, 16, 17 and 18 years, size 16 requiring 3 yards 42-inch material with 1 yard 36-inch contrasting goods and 1 yard of 27-inch lining. Price 15 cents.

8512—Ladies' and Misses' long cape, gathered to a small yoke, with a flaring Medici or round collar, with or without a fitted vest. Cuts in 4 sizes 32, 36, 40 and 44 inches bust measure, size 36 requiring 3½ yards 54-inch material with ⅞ yard 30-inch contrasting material and ⅞ yard 27-inch lining for vest. Price 15 cents.

8514—Ladies' and Misses' Basque waist to be made high or V-neck, with standing or Medici collar and full-length sleeves having circular frills. Pattern cuts in sizes 32 to 44 inches bust measure, size 36 requiring 2¾ yards 36-inch material with ½ yard 27-inch contrasting material and 2 yards 27-inch lining. Price 15 cents.

8527—Ladies' and Misses' waist with Medici collar, inset vest, removable chemisette and full-length sleeves. Pattern cuts in sizes 34 to 46 inches bust measure, size 36 requiring 2⅞ yards 27-inch material with ⅞ yard 27-inch contrasting material Price 15 cents.

8545—Ladies' and Misses' sash waist with inset vest, Medici collar or pointed collar. Cuts in sizes 34 to 44 inches bust measure, size 36 requiring 2¼ yards 36-inch material with ⅝ yard 13-inch or wider all-over lace for vest and ¾ yard 30-inch contrasting goods for collars and vest. Price 15 cents.

8562—Ladies' and Misses' waist consisting of a kimono guimpe with Medici collar and flaring cuffs, and a Basque overblouse. Cuts in sizes 32 to 42 inches bust measure, requiring in size 36, 1 yard 72-inch net for guimpe and 1½ yards 27-inch contrasting material for overblouse. Price 15 cents.

8565—Ladies' and Misses' waist opening in front with wide corselet girdle, slashed shawl collar and one-piece full-length sleeves. Cuts in sizes 32 to 44 inches bust measure. Size 36 requires 1⅝ yards 30-inch material with ⅜ yard 36-inch contrasting satin. Price 15 cents.

8512
Emb. 14600

8465
Emb. 14185

8545
Emb. 14286
Emb. 14504

8463
Emb. 14687

8514   Emb. 14548   8565   Emb. 14303   8527   Emb. 14196   8562   Emb. 14606

14600—Pine-cone border. This design may be used as a border or as separate motifs. 2¼ inches wide, 3 yards in the pattern. 10 cents.

14548—Floral sprays. These are appropriate for embroidering waists, dresses, négligées and underwear. Pattern contains 12 sprays in 5 sizes. 15 cents.

14303—Conventional border. Effective for embroidering waists, dresses, evening wraps and suits of silk, wool or linen. One or more colors may be used. 3¼ inches wide, 3 yards. 15 cents.

14286—Dainty sprays for embroidering neckwear, waists and children's clothes in solid work and eyelets. Pattern contains 8 sprays. 10 cents.

14504—Braiding border. 3 inches wide, 3 yards and 4 corners. This may be carried out in cord, braid or chain-stitch. 10 cents.

14687—Sheet of sprays and large eyelets for trimming waists, dresses, neckwear, négligées and underwear. These sprays are attractive developed in colors in solid work. 10 cents.

14196—Sheet of 9 sprays. They may be carried out in French and eyelet work on waists, dresses, underwear and children's clothes. 10 cents.

14606—Bulgarian borders for outline-stitch, cable-stitch or snail trail. Pattern contains three different designs; ½, ⅝ and ¾ inches wide. 3 yards and 4 corners of each are given. 10 cents.

14185—Braiding borders. 1¾ and 2½ inches wide, respectively, 2¼ yards of each are given. Suitable for trimming dresses, suits and evening wraps. 15 cents.

DAINTY LITTLE DESIGNS FOR EMBROIDERING CHILDREN'S SCHOOL AND PLAY FROCKS

8347   8541

8442   8469

8553

8497

8553
Emb. 14498

8497
Emb. 14680

8347
Emb. 14417

8541
Emb. 14406

8442
Emb. 14418

8469
Emb. 14387

INDIVIDUALITY may be given to the simplest of frocks by a touch of hand embroidery, such as pattern 14417, which is illustrated on dress 8347. This pattern contains five wreaths, in three different styles, suitable for embroidering lingerie dresses, waists, and underwear in solid work and eyelets in white or blue mercerized cotton. The dress pattern is cut in nine sizes; ½, 1, 2, 3, 4, 6, 8, 10 and 12 years. 10 cents each.

14406—This simple scalloped border is appropriate for use on underwear, children's clothes, neckwear, waists, underwear and négligées, as well as small table linens. The pattern contains two borders, ⅜ and ⅝ inch wide, 3 yards and 4 corners of each are given in the pattern. 10 cents. The narrower border is illustrated on suit 8541, which is cut in five sizes; ½, 1, 2, 3 and 4 years. 15 cents.

14418—This dainty design of flower sprays may be used for embroidering children's rompers, dresses, waists, underwear and infants' garments. The pattern contains 6 sprays, which may be developed in solid work and eyelets with white mercerized cotton. The largest spray is illustrated on rompers 8442, which are cut in six sizes; ½ to 6 years inclusive. The transfer pattern and rompers pattern are each 10 cents.

14387—Appropriate is this simple scalloped border for finishing the edges of collars and vests of boys' suits, as well as trimming underwear, négligées and household linens. It may be developed in white or a color. It is ½ inch wide and 6 yards and 4 corners are contained in the pattern for 10 cents. The suit 8469, on which the scalloped edging is shown, comes in 4, 6, 8, 10 and 12 years. 15 cents.

14498—Delicate pink, blue and green may be used in developing this cross-stitch design, which is two inches wide. This border is appropriate for trimming children's dresses, caps, aprons and fancy articles, and it is illustrated on dress 8553, which is cut in four sizes; 2, 4, 6 and 8 years. 15 cents. Three yards of cross-stitch border are contained in the transfer pattern for 10 cents.

14680—Solid work, outline and couched cord are all suitable for carrying out this simple design in two colors or two shades of one color. This border is 2 inches wide and 3 yards and 4 corners are given for 10 cents. This design is suitable for trimming dresses, coats or suits of linen, silk, wool or crêpe materials, and it is illustrated on dress 8497 which comes in sizes 6, 8, 10, 12 and 14 years. 15 cents.

ATTRACTIVE EMBROIDERY DESIGNS SUITABLE FOR DECORATING SIMPLE UNDERWEAR

8408   8272   7852 8105   7267   6148 8540

8408
Emb. 14515

8272
Emb. 14505

7852-8105
Emb. 14439-14630

7267
Emb. 14667-14478

6148-8540
Emb. 14133-14477

14478—This plain scalloped border, used for finishing the neck of nightgown 7267, may also be used on underwear, neckwear, waists, dresses and children's clothes, as well as small household linens. It is ½-inch wide and 6 yards and 4 corners are given in the pattern for 10 cents.

14133—The wild rose and forget-me-not design for a corset-cover may also be used for embroidering a chemise or nightgown, by using border 14134, which is 4 inches wide and 2¼ yards long, for the bottom of the garment or sleeves. 15 cents each. This design, illustrated on corset-cover 6148, comes in sizes 32 to 44 inches. 10 cents.

14477—This plain scalloped border, which is ¼-inch wide, is shown on the envelope drawers 8540, which comes in sizes 22 to 34 inches. 6 yards and 4 corners of scalloped border are contained in pattern. 10 cents each.

SIMPLE designs in hand embroidery are often as effective as more elaborate ones. The beading design, 14515, is illustrated on princess slip 8408, which comes in sizes 32 to 46 inches. 15 cents. The large eyelets and wreaths are suitable for use on underwear, nightgowns and children's clothes. This pattern is 2¼ inches wide and 3 yards are given for 10 cents.

14505—This scalloped border for eyelet work may be adapted in many ways for embroidering underwear, négligées, waists and dresses, as well as household linens. It is 5½ inches wide and 2¼ yards are given in the pattern. This design makes an attractive trimming for the combination garment, 8272, which comes in sizes 32 to 42 inches. 15 cents each.

14439—The attractive beading, illustrated on corset-cover 7852, is one of 4 designs contained in this pattern, which may be used for embroidering underwear, neckwear and chil-

dren's dresses and aprons. The wide border, on the flounce of petticoat 8105, might be used with this design for embroidering combination garments. This daisy border, 14630, is 4 inches wide and 2¼ yards are given in the pattern. The corset-cover is cut in sizes 32, 34, 36, 38, 40, 42 and 44 inches, and the petticoat comes in sizes 22, 24, 26, 28, 30, 32 and 34 inches. 15 cents each.

14667—These attractive butterflies are suitable for embroidering nightgowns, underwear, négligées, lingerie dresses, waists and chiffon evening gowns, as well as lingerie pillows, bureau-scarfs, tea-cloths, and sideboard covers. This design may be developed in white on fine lawn, batiste or handkerchief linen in solid work, eyelets, outline and seed-stitch, or in beads on chiffon. This pattern includes two large butterflies, each 10 by 12 inches and 3 smaller ones, each 6¼ by 8 inches. They are illustrated on nightgown 7267 which is cut in sizes 32 to 44 inches. 15 cents each.

14676— Four stencil designs (at left.) These hollyhock motifs are each 16 by 5¼ inches. Price 15 cents.

14123— Six stencil designs. The border, illustrated on the curtain, is 11½ inches high. Price 15 cents.

14676— Daisy design for a pillow, 16-inches square, and three different designs for stenciling pillows, runners and curtains of Russian crash, linen, scrim, rep or pongee. Outline-stitch and darning may be used. Price 15 cents.

14123

14675— Dogwood design for a pillow. Pattern also includes a tulip border 8-inches high. Price 15 cents.

14674— Fleur-de-lis design and rose corner for stenciling or embroidery. Price 15 cents.

14674

14674

14002— Conventional flower design. Price 15 cents.

14583

14686— Tray design for colored embroidery. 15 by 16 inches. Price 10 cents.

14583 — Swedish design for table-cover, 27-inches square. Price 15 cents.

14297— Doily design 6½ inches in diameter, 4 transfers given. Price 10 cents.

14614— Two table-mat designs for embroidery and cut leather. Price 15 cents.

14686

14684— Two motifs for runners, pillow-covers or screens. Price 15 cents.

14619 — Chinese motifs, 4½ and 7 inches, 4 of each. Price 15 cents.

14685 — Design for between-meals-mat. 22-inches in diameter. Price 15 cents.

14614— Two table-mat designs for embroidery and cut leather. Price 15 cents.

14684

14297

14619

14614

14614

Patterns 14674, 14675 and 14676 were illustrated on page 84 of May Ladies' Home Journal.

Patterns 14684, 14685 and 14686 were illustrated on page 28 of August Ladies' Home Journal.

14685

SIMPLE AND ATTRACTIVE DESIGNS FOR USE ON PRACTICAL GIFTS

14666

14665

14666

14666

14665

14352—Seven stencil motifs. These conventional designs may be used as allover patterns or repeated to form borders for decorating sideboard-scarfs, pillows, runners, table-covers, couch-covers, screens, curtains, portières, lamp-shades, candle-shades, and waste-baskets. The sideboard-scarf, illustrated here, was of natural colored linen, stenciled in dark blue and green, and the candle-shades were of china silk, made over a frame, and stenciled with the same colorings. 15 cents.

NOTE:—Patterns 14665 and 14666 were illustrated on page 35 of March Ladies' Home Journal.

14665

14666—Five wedgewood designs. Suitable for embroidering trays, covers for a hand-glass, waste-basket, card-cases, belt-buckle, bags and many other articles. These designs may be developed in ribbon, or filo silk in white or colors. An initial may be placed in the center of the designs on the card cases. 15 cents.

14666

14665—Six wedgewood designs. These may be developed in solid work, outline-stitch, eyelets and feather-stitching, in white or delicate colors. The flowers and leaves are effective developed in ribbon work, the stems in filo silk and the bow-knots in couched cord. Ribbon work is rapidly done as one stitch forms a petal or leaf. 15 cents.

14665

14118—Five stencil designs. Suitable for decorating screens, portières, curtains, couch-covers, pillows and runners, in one or more colors. They may be used to form allover patterns or borders. 15 cents.

ATTRACTIVE DESIGNS FOR HOUSEHOLD LINENS

14334

14332

14334—Snow-drop design for a 22-inch towel of huckaback or damask. Transfers for stamping two towels, with scallops for both ends, are included in the pattern. 10 cents.

14399—Eyelet border adapted to a luncheon cloth. The pattern includes two yards of border, 7½ inches wide, which may also be adapted to a sideboard cover, bureau-scarf, vestibule curtains, or used as a trimming for lingerie dresses. 15 cents.

12780

14332—Towel design 22 inches long. Pattern contains scallops for both ends of two towels. 10 cents.

12780—Four sprays, 6 by 11 inches, for embroidering a set of bed linens. 15 cents.

14458—Daisy sprays adapted to a luncheon-cloth. 4 sprays in pattern, 2, 10 by 10½ inches and 2, 7½ by 9¾ inches. Suitable for embroidering bed or table-linen. 15 cents.

14399

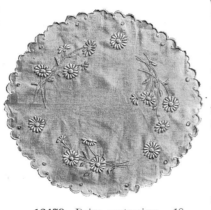

13479—Daisy centerpiece. 18 inches in diameter. Bread-and-butter plate doilies, number 13481 may be used with this design. 15 cents.

14458

14574

14543

14091

14574—Border for eyelet work, beads or embroidery, 2¼ inches wide, 3 yards in the pattern. This border is suitable for use on bureau-scarfs, tray-cloths and dresses. 15 cents.

14543—Three designs for guest-towels. Each 18 inches long. These designs should be embroidered in white in solid work and eyelets, and a two-inch initial may be placed in the center of each design. Scallops for finishing both ends of each towel are included in the pattern. 15 cents.

14091—Design for a towel. It may also be adapted to pillow-cases or a bureau-scarf. This design is 24 inches long, and the pattern includes transfers for stamping both ends of two towels. This design may be developed in solid work and eyelets, in white. 10 cents.

14335—Floral border adapted to a towel. Pattern contains 3 yards and 4 corners of border 3¼ inches wide, 1½ yards reversed. This design may be used on towels, pillow cases, sheets or bureau-scarfs. 10 cents.

14525—Seven simple designs for embroidering guest-towels. The darning and cross-stitch borders should be developed in colors and the buttonhole edges done in white. One yard of each border is given in the pattern. 10 cents.

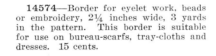

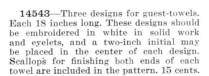

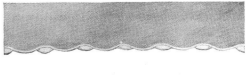

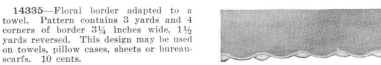

14525

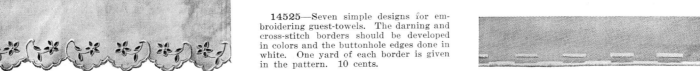

STENCILING, BATIK, AND BLOCK PRINTING

14157—Suitable for use in living room or veranda

14299—Stenciled in soft shades of pink and green on grey linen

14352—Stenciled on a table runner and lamp shade

STENCILING is so easy to do, so artistic, when well done, and so inexpensive a method of decorating cheap materials, that it is no longer a fad but an accepted style of decoration. It is to be used on pillows, candle-shades, tea-trays, table-covers, curtains, portières, runners and many fancy articles, suitable for Christmas gifts or fairs.

In choosing your design, remember that fine delicate patterns should not be used on heavy, coarse materials, as Russian crash, Monk's cloth, burlap or crafts canvas; or coarse designs on fine delicate materials. First transfer your design to the stencil board. If you do not have a stencil board, thin bristol board or even very heavy wrapping paper may be used. If wrapping paper is used, however, it is a good plan to varnish it on both sides after the design has been cut out, to make it more durable. A simple stencil design, having fairly large holes, may be cut with small, sharp scissors, but it is always better to cut out these designs with a knife. While cutting the design it is best to put the stencil paper on a piece of glass or sheet of metal. Your knife should be very sharp and large enough to hold with a firm grip in an upright position. If the point of the knife becomes dull, sharpen it before going on with your work, as you cannot cut a stencil with a dull knife.

When a stencil is once cut it may be used any number of times and may be moved along to form a border or an allover pattern. Place your material over a large blotter on a table and place the cut stencil in the desired position, then fasten it down with thumb tacks so that the color medium cannot run under the edges.

Have as many bristle brushes as you are to use colors and use one brush for each color. These brushes should be cut off to within ¼ inch of the ferrules. Dip the brush in the paint and before applying it to the stencil, rub it almost dry on another piece of cloth; there will be enough paint left on the brush to use for stenciling. Rub the color so thoroughly into the fabric that no paint will be left on the surface as the design should have the appearance of being woven into the material.

Now as to the colors: If one understands the mixing of colors, almost any shade of any color can be made with a little experimenting, from the following list: Alazarin crimson, permanent blue, chrome yellow, burnt sienna, vermilion, black and white. If you do not understand the mixing of colors, it is best to buy the shades of oil paint you wish, already mixed. The ordinary artist's oil colors mixed with gasoline or with a preparation of turpentine, 1 pint, acetic acid, one ounce, oil of wintergreen, 1 ounce, make a satisfactory color medium, and if either of these are used the article can be washed when it becomes soiled. Only enough of the medium should be used to dilute the paint to the consistency of cream.

Have the colors harmonious with the tone of the ma-

14475—A runner for the nursery

terial and with each other. This can be done by putting a tiny bit of each color into each of the others. It is much better to use two shades of one color or two colors than several colors for doing this work.

BLOCK PRINTING.

Block Printing is another easy and artistic method of decorating materials. It has much the same effect as stenciling, except that in block printing the coloring matter is on the surface of the material instead of having the effect of being woven in it. The design should be transferred to a smooth block of soft wood. Cut away the background of the design with a sharp penknife and small chisel. This will leave the design in relief.

Any small design suitable for stenciling can also be used as a block print, but it is advisable for the begin-

14415—A table-cover of linen, stenciled in reds, greens, brown and blue

ner to select a simple design without many small spaces, as it is easier to cut away the background. If two colors are to be used the coloring matter should be put on the block with a brush, but if one color is to be used saturate a pad of cotton or cloth with oil paint in the desired color. This should be mixed with a preparation for fixing the color in the material, as for stenciling, and should be about the consistency of cream. This is made by mixing turpentine one pint, acetic acid one ounce, and oil of wintergreen one ounce. Stamp the block first on the saturated pad, then on the material, repeating the design to form an allover pattern or border as may be desired. The block may be used innumerable times for decorating curtains, pillows, table-covers, counterpanes, also kimonos and dresses. Block printing should be used on loosely woven materials, which will absorb the coloring matter, not on poplin or denim. Crafts canvas, Russian crash and pongee are good materials for this work. This block printing is used in making Japanese and India prints.

This process is used by the Japanese in making many of their beautiful figured fabrics, and while it may seem difficult to the beginner, it has so many possibilities of development that it is well worth while.

BATIK MAKING.

This is done by dyeing the background of the design, leaving the design in the natural color of the material. Loosely woven fabrics, such as linen, pongee or un-

bleached cotton should be used for this work. Transfer the design to the material, then go over the design with melted wax, painting it on to completely cover the material. This may be put on with a brush. Only coarse designs should be used for this batik making. When the wax has cooled and dried into the material, dip the material into a cold dye of the desired color. Dyes that have been boiled, then cooled, vegetable dyes, or oil paint mixed with gasoline, may be used. When the material has thoroughly dried and the gasoline has evaporated, wash the material with soap and warm water, washing out the wax and leaving the design in original color of the material. Indigo, brown, soft dull reds and orange are the best colors to use for this work. Part of the design may be stenciled afterward if one likes. Table-covers, pillows, runners and bags may be decorated in this way.

14157—Design for a settee-back or cushion. Six motifs in the pattern, each 6¾ by 11 inches. These may be developed in stencil, batik, block printing, appliqué or outline-stitch and darning. These motifs are also effective for decorating portières, couch-covers, or runners of crafts canvas, Monk's cloth or cotton velour. 15 cents.

14299—Seven stencil designs. The snow-ball design, stenciled on the centerpiece is 13¼ by 5½ inches; the apple corner for a table-cover is 7 by 7 inches; flower sprays, 6 by 3 inches; tulip design for ends of a runner, 13¼ by 11 inches; edelweiss motif, suitable for curtains, bags and novelties, is 6 by 4 inches; tudor rose corner is 8½ by 8½ inches and conventional design 9 by 6½ inches. Any of these motifs may be used for decorating curtains, table-covers and pillows. 15 cents.

14352—Seven stencil motifs. These conventional designs may be carried out in stencil, batik or block printing on runners, lamp-shades, pillows, table-covers, screens, curtains, portières or waste-baskets. They may be used as allover patterns or borders. 15 cents.

14415—Five Turkish stencils. These designs are appropriate for stenciling curtains, table-covers, tea-tray, couch-covers, portières and sofa-pillows in Oriental colors, using blue, red, brown and green. Crafts canvas, Russian crash, Egyptian cloth, scrim, linen and pongee are suitable materials on which to use these designs. 15 cents.

14475—Bear designs for stencil or appliqué. Five designs in the pattern. These motifs are appropriate for decorating the curtains, pillows and covers in a child's room. If stenciled, they may be accentuated by outlining them in black, or a darker shade of the color used. 15 cents.

14415—An artistic tea-tray of stenciled linen, covered with glass and framed

USEFUL ACCESSORIES TO BE EMBROIDERED

14422—Two designs for bags. This design may be used for bag or handkerchief case. The flap is 4 by 9¾ inches. 10 cents.

13314—This motif is three inches high and may be developed in solid work or appliqué. Two yards are given. 10 cents.

14448—Three designs for embroidering bags. They may be developed in embroidery, braid and stencil on bags of silk or velvet. 10 cents.

14422—Two designs for bags. This dainty design may be developed in solid and eyelet work on linen. It is 5½ by 6½ inches. 10 cents.

14177   14030   14110   14049   14285

14177—Seven attractive sprays of lily of the valley for 10 cents.
14030—Design of dots. Four motifs given in pattern. 15 cents.
14110—Three floral designs for hosiery. 6 transfers. 10 cents.
14049—Sheet of butterfly designs in various sizes. 10 cents.
14285—Six bow-knot designs, 33 transfers in pattern. 10 cents.

14379—*Four designs for handkerchiefs.* These should be stamped on the finest of handkerchief linen or lawn, and embroidered in white or a color, in solid work or eyelets. 10 cents.

14423—*Design for a bag,* 9½ by 9 inches. May be embroidered in solid or eyelet work on linen, Russian crash or pongee. Cutting outline is contained in pattern. 10 cents.

14423

14114

14277—*Four designs for handkerchiefs.* These designs may be embroidered in French and eyelet work, and initials in ½-inch size may be placed in the wreaths. 10 cents.

14114—*Eight squares in Richelieu embroidery* which may be used on bags or household linens. They are attractive worked on heavy linen and connected by strips of Cluny lace. 15 cents.

14645—*Goldenrod design for an apron,* 9½ inches long, 21 inches wide. Should be developed in solid work and French knots in colors. 15 cents.

14380—*Five designs for handkerchiefs;* 12 inches square. An initial or monogram may be placed in one corner of each handkerchief. 10 cents.

14647—*Design for an apron with pockets.* When not in use, the top may be folded in and drawn up to form a bag. 15 cents.

ATTRACTIVE ACCESSORIES IN CROCHET

KEY—Ch. means chain ; sc. means single crochet ; dc. means double crochet ; tr. c. means treble crochet (wrap twice) ; sl. st., slip stitch ; fd., foundation ; x is sign of repetition.

No. 9. Directions for Picot-Edge Lace

Material requirements : No. 70 D.M.C. and No. 13 steel hook. Start with 19 ch., turn.

1st row.—sc. in 9th ch. from needle, 5 ch., sc. in 14th ch., 5 ch., sc. in 1st foundation ch., 6 ch., turn.

2nd row.—sc. over 1st loop, 5 ch., sc. over 2nd loop, 5 ch., sc. in 3rd ch. at end, 7 ch., turn.

3rd row.—sc. over 1st loop, 5 ch., sc. over 2nd loop, 5 ch., sc. in 3rd ch. at end, 3 ch., turn.

4th row.—3 (5-ch.) picots, 8 dc. in 1st loop, 1 sc. (to form shell), 7 dc. in 2nd loop, 1 sc., 5 dc. in 3rd loop, 1 dc. in 4th ch. at end, 6 ch., turn.

5th row.—sc. in 4th dc. (of shell), 5 ch., sc. in 4th of 2nd shell, 5 ch., sc. in 4th dc. of 3rd shell, 6 ch., turn.

6th row.—Repeat, beginning with second row, to end of lace (finishing with row of shells).

Directions for top edge.—Fasten thread, 5 ch., x 1 dc. in 1st loop, 2 ch., 1 dc. in 2nd loop, 2 ch., 1 dc. in 1st dc. of shell, 2 ch. x repeat from star to end of lace.

No. 10. Fish Net Lace With Picot-Edge Loop

Use No. 70 cotton, No. 13 hook.

Start with 16 ch., turn. 1st row.—x dc. in 3rd ch., 9 dc. in next 9 chs., 5 ch., turn.

2nd row.—sc. in 4th dc., 5 ch., sc. in 6th dc., 5 ch., sc. in 8th dc., 5 ch., sc. in 10th dc., 5 ch., sc. over 2 ch. st. at end of row of dc., 5 ch., sc., on opposite side of row in 3rd dc., 5 ch., sc. in 5th dc., 5 ch., sc. in 7th dc., 3 ch., x sc. in 1st foundation ch., turn.

3rd row.—5 ch., sc. in 2nd loop, 5 ch., sc. in 3rd loop, 5 ch., sc. in 4th loop, 5 ch., x tr.c. in 5th loop, 4 ch.-pc. x repeat four times, skipping pc. on 5th tr.c., 5 ch., sc. in 1st loop on opposite side, 5 ch., sc. in 2nd loop, 5 ch., sc. in 3rd loop, 5 ch., sc. in 4th loop.

4th row.—x 19 ch., turn, repeat from x in 1st row to x in 2nd row, sc. in 3rd st. of 19 ch., 3 ch., sc. in first loop opposite, 3 ch., sc. back in 2nd loop of point just being completed, 3 ch., sc. in 2nd loop opposite, 3 ch., sc. back in 3rd loop of point just being completed, 5 ch., sc. in 4th loop, 5 ch., x tr.c. in 5th loop, 4 ch.-pc. x repeat four times, skipping pc. on 5th tr.c., 5 ch., sc. in 1st loop on opposite side, 5 ch., sc. in 2nd loop, 5 ch., sc. in 3rd loop, 5 ch., sc. in 4th loop. Repeat from x at beginning of 4th row to end of lace, turn.

Top Edge : 1st row.—6 ch., sc. in 1st loop, x 3 ch., sc. in next loop, x repeat to end.

2nd row.—3 ch., sc. over each 3 chs. in 1st row, repeat to end.

3rd row.—4 ch., dc. in 5th ch. from needle, x 1 ch., skip 1st., 1 dc. x repeat to end.

No. 11. Star Wheel Lace

Material Requirements : No. 70 D.M.C. No. 13 needle. Start with 8 ch., join.

1st row.—5 ch., 1 dc. in 1st ch. of circle, 3 ch., 1 dc. in next ch. of circle, repeat until 7 loops are made, 3 ch., join to form 8th loop, 1 ch.

2nd row.—5 sc. in each loop, join with sl. st.

3rd row.—6 ch., join with sc. in every 5th sc., directly over each dc. in 1st row of dc.'s, making 8 loops, 1 ch.

4th row.—9 sc. in each loop. This completes the x. Make 2nd x and join to 1st x by sl. st. after 5th sc. in each of last two loops to 5th sc. in two loops in 1st x. Continue from beginning to end of lace.

Directions for top edge of lace : 1st row.—Fasten thread to 5th sc. of loop in star, 1 sl. st. x 6 ch., sl. st. in 5th sc. of 2nd loop, 9 ch., sl. st. in 5th sc. x repeat from x to end of lace, 1 ch., turn.

2nd row.—sc. in each ch. of 1st row. 4 ch., turn.

3rd row.—1 dc. in 2nd sc., x skip 1 sc., 1 ch., 1 dc. in next sc. x repeat from x to end, turn.

4th row.—6 ch., sc. over 3rd space, sc. over 4th space, x 6 ch., skip 1 space, sc. over next space, sc. over next space, x repeat from x to end, turn.

5th row.—9 sc. in each loop to end, 8 ch., turn.

6th row.—Sl. st. in 5th sc. of loop, x 6 ch., sl. st. in 5th sc. of next loop, x repeat from x to end of lace, turn.

7th row.—4 ch., 1 dc. in 6th ch. from needle, x 1 ch., skip 1 st. and dc. in next ch., x repeat to end of lace, 1 ch., turn.

8th row.—1 sc. in each ch.

No. 3. Irish Picot Coat Collar. No. 60 cotton and No. 10 Eagle crochet hook.

1st ring : Commence with 12 ch. join to form ring. Over this ring make 3 sc. 3 ch. and repeat 4 times. This finishes first loop. 15 ch. fasten to the 2nd stitch from last loop. This makes another ring. Over this make 3 sc. 2 ch. fasten to first picot on first loop. 2 ch. 3 sc. 3 ch. 3 sc. 3 ch. 2 sc. 10 ch. turn and fasten between the last two picots. Turn, 3 sc. 3 ch. Repeat 4 times, 1 sc. into the lower loop, 3 ch. 3 sc. 3 ch. 3 sc. This finishes the 2 loops, one over the other. Now chain 15 and fasten as before to the 2nd stitch from last loop. Over this ring crochet 3 sc. 2 ch. fasten to first picot on opposite loop, 2 ch. 3 sc. 3 ch. 3 sc. 3 ch. 2 sc. 10 ch. Turn and fasten between the 2 picots, 3 sc. 2 ch. Fasten to first picot on second loop, 2 ch. 3 sc. 3 ch. 3 sc. 3 ch. 2 sc. 10 ch. Fasten between the 2 picots, 3 sc. 3 ch. Repeat 4 times, 1 sc., 3 ch. 3 sc. 3 ch. 3 sc. into next loop 1 sc. 3 ch. 3 sc. 3 ch. 3 sc. into next loop ; this makes three loops one over the other. Add one loop to each row until you have 9 loops. Next row, 8 loops ; next row, 7 loops, then 8, then 9, then 8, then 7, repeat this 4 times and end with 9, 8, 7, 6, 5, 4, 3, 2, 1 loops.

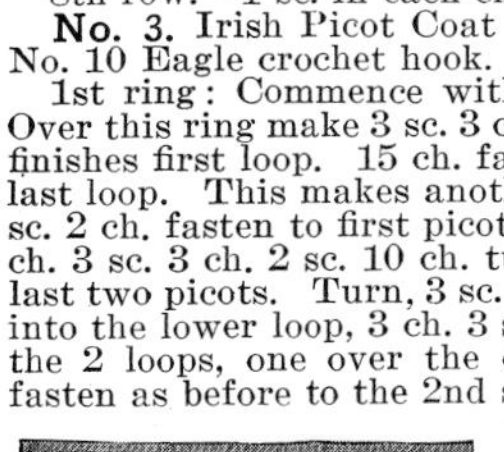

No. 11

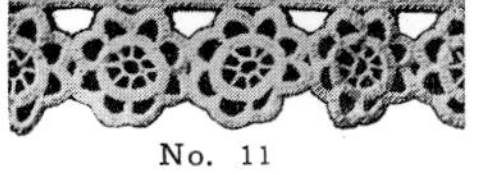

No. 9

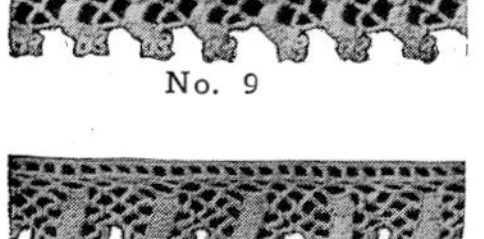

No. 10

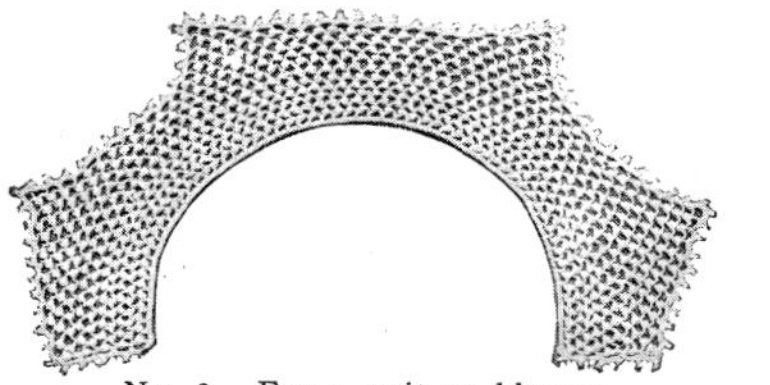

No. 3. For a suit or blouse.

No. 8. Crocheted Moccasins

Material requirements : 2 balls No. 6 Macramé Cord, crochet needle No. 5.

Chain 55. Work around this with sc. 5 times, widening at each end. Then continue widening at one end 4 times around for the toe ; then 4 times around, not widening. Then narrow at toe 4 times around vamp.

Top piece : Chain 14. Work around this 11 times, widening at each end enough to keep it flat. Then sew to the other part on sides and around toe.

Continue heighth of moccasin by two rows sc. from right end of vamp (around heel) to left end and fasten thread tightly.

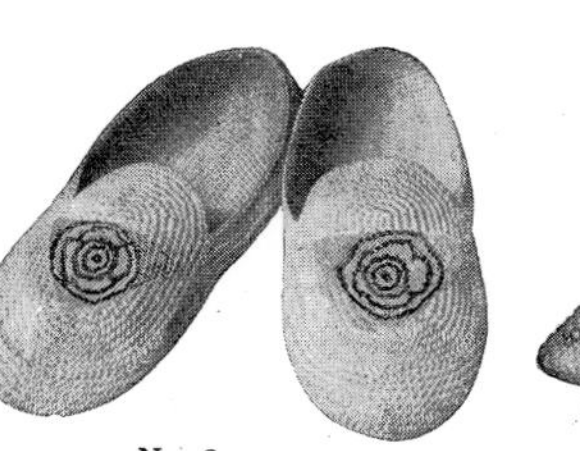

No. 8

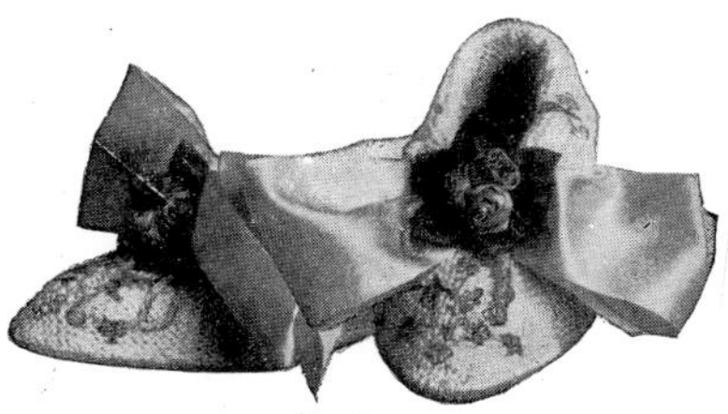

No. 7

This will form a moccasin No. 6. For larger sizes, 2 extra foundation chains for each half size.

Rose designs : To make the central raised part of rose wind padding thread (or Macramé cord) around little finger 10 times, slip windings from finger and crochet over them sc. stitches closely as possible and as many as wheel will contain (24 in all). Ch. 4 and join to ring. Repeat this 4 times, making 5 ch. loops. Work into each of these ch. loops 1 sc. and 7 dc., completing 5 petals.

2nd row.—Ch. 5 and join in back of dc. of each of 5 petals. Work into each of these ch. loops, 1 dc. and 10 tr.c.

3rd row.—Ch. 7 and join in back of dc. of each of 5 petals. Work into each of these ch. loops, 1 dc. and 13 tr.c.

No. 7. Blue Knit Slippers

1 skein of light blue D.M.C. Mercerized Cotton, No. 3. 1 knot or lap of white D.M.C. Mercerized Cotton No. 3. 1 pair pointed blue satin quilted soles. Work embroidery in colors in cross-stitch.

Colors two shades of blue, pink, green and one of yellow. $1\frac{1}{2}$ yards of blue satin ribbon $2\frac{1}{2}$ or 3 inches wide.

With the white D.M.C. take up twenty stitches on medium size knitting needles and knit across twenty times, making a square, then tie on blue and knit until you have it long enough to reach around the sole, join to white square. Knit a piece of white ten stitches wide and sew on the blue as a turn-over. Then embroider the flowers on the white toe and the narrow over pieces. After sewing the soles, finish with bows of blue ribbon and rosettes of silk flowers made of odd bits of silk.

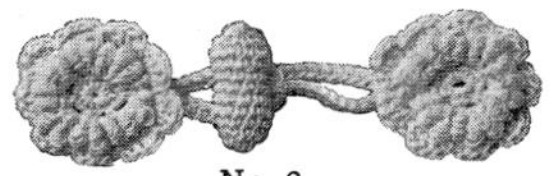

No. 2

No 2. Coat Ornament

Use Cordonnet No 5, No. 8 Needle.

Ch. 4, join. 6 sc. in ring, join. 3 ch., 1 sc. in each st., making 6 loops, ch. 3. Then 3 roll stitches in each loop, making 18 roll sts.

(To make roll stitch.) Wind thread around needle 9 times, thread over needle, draw through 9 loops on needle, ch. 1, and repeat.

1 sc. between each roll stitch, join. Ch. 3, miss 1 sc., 1 sc. in next stitch. Repeat, making 9 loops of 3 ch., 4 dc. in each loop and 1 sc. between. Sl. st. to back of scallop and ch. 25, turn, and 24 sc. on ch., fasten to back of scallop.

Make another and join to this one.

To make the button : Ch. 3, join. 6 sc. in the 3 ch., 2 sc. in each sc. Repeat the 16 sc. for five rows, then sl. st. to center of loop on medallion. Then 5 more rows and fill with cotton, sc. in every other st. until closed.

No. 1. Crocheted Bag.—s.c., single crochet—that is—without throwing thread over. l.c., long crochet —that is—thread over twice.

Materials—5 balls Crochet Cotton No. 3. 3 yards white cord. No. 9 hook, ¼ yard silk for lining.

The roll stitch of which the bag is formed is made as follows : Roll the thread 10 times around the hook ; insert the hook under loop to be filled ; throw thread over the hook and draw through the entire roll which is on the hook ; throw thread over the hook and draw through the loop, and repeat for next stitch.

Make a chain of 180 stitches and join the ends.

1st row.—Chain 5, skip five, s.c. into next stitch and repeat around the circle, when there should be 60 loops of 5 chain.

2nd row.—Chain 5, s.c. into first 5 chain of previous row ; 6 roll stitches into second 5 chain ; s.c. into third 5 chain ; and repeat around the circle, when there should be twelve shells, with loops of 5 chain between.

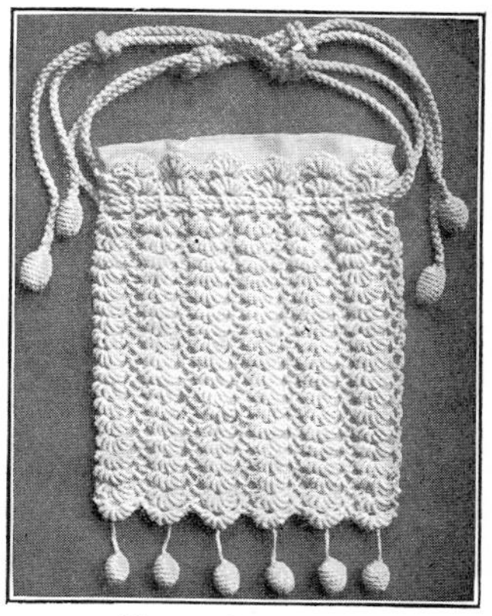

No. 1. Crocheted bag in wheat stitch.

3rd row.—Reverse the work. Chain 5 ; s.c. into first 5 chain of previous row ; chain 5 s.c. between second and third roll stitches of shell ; chain 5, s.c. between fourth and fifth roll stitches ; chain 5 s.c. into next 5 chain of previous row ; and repeat around the circle.

4th row.—Reverse the work and proceed as in second row.

5th row.—Same as third row.

Continue the work until you have eighteen rows of shells, or as deep as you desire to make the bag.

With the work folded wrong side out, join the bottom edges with single crochet around the shells.

To make the beading for drawing cords, attach the thread to the top, and chain 4 ; 1 l.c. into first chain loop of first row ; chain 4, skip one chain loop, l.c. into next chain loop ; repeat around the bag.

Around this beading crochet two rows of shells, same as the lower part of the bag, and finish the edge as follows : Chain 3, s.c. between first two roll stitches, chain 3, s.c. between next two roll stitches, and repeat around the top.

Make the balls as follows : Chain 5, join the ends ; fill this circle with alternate s.c. and 1 chain.

2nd row.—2 s.c. alternated with 1 chain ; then six rows around with s.c. and no chain. Pack the ball tightly with absorbent cotton, and continue the s.c., narrowing to the top ; finishing with ten chain, for attaching the ball to the shell.

For the cords.—when the ball is nearly completed, insert the end of the cord into the opening, crochet around it and fasten the thread securely.

The reason for reversing the work between the rows is that the rows of shells may go straight around the bag,—not spirally.

The bag is very pretty made of colored thread, lined with a contrasting color ; for instance,—black lined with emerald green ; or écru lined with brown.

No. 4. Measures 22 s. across. Work a foundation of 54 ch. At the end of each row, add 5 ch. to turn. 1st r. 1 t. into 8th ch., 21 s. = 22 spaces. 2nd r. 22 s. 3rd r. 10 s., 5 t., 10 s. 4th r. 10 s., 9 t., 9 s. 5th r. 6 s., 5 t., 1 s., 5 t., 1 s., 5t., 1s., 5 t., 6s. 6th r. 6 s., 9 t., 1 s., 9 t., 1 s., 9 t., 5s. 7th r. 5s., 5 t., 1 s., 5 t., 1 s., 5 t., 1 s., 5 t., 1 s., 5 t., 5 s. 8th r. 6s., 9 t., 2 ch., 3 t., with 2 ch. in between into the same space, 3 ch., 3 t. with 2 ch. in between into the same space, 1 s., 9 t., 5 s. 9th r. 3 s., 5 t., 1 s., 5 t., 1 s., 3 ch., 3 t., with 2 ch in between into the same space ; 3 ch., 1 t., 1s., 5 t., 1 s., 5 t., 3s. 10th r. 3 s., 9 t., 3 s., 3 ch., 3 t. with 2 ch. in between into the same space, 3 ch., 3 t., with 2 ch. in between into the same space ; 3 ch., 1 t., 3 s., 9 t., 2 s. 11th r. 2s., 5 t., 1 s., 5 t., 3 ch., 3 t., with 2 ch. in between into the same space, 3 ch., 3 t. with 2 ch. in between into the same space ; 3 ch., 3 t. with 2 ch. in between into the same space ; 3 ch., 1 t., 5 t., 1 s., 5 t., 2 s. 12th r. 3 s., 9 t., 2 ch., 3 t. with 2 ch. in between into the same space ; 3 ch., 3 t. with 2 ch. in between into the same space ; 3 ch., 3 t. with 2 ch. in between into the same space ; 3 ch., 3 t. with 2 ch. in between into the same space ; 1 s., 9 t., 2 s. 13th r. 3 s., 5 t., 1 s., 5 t., 1 s., 3 ch., 3 t. with 2 ch. in between into the same space ; 3 ch., 1 t., 1 s., 5 t., 1 s., 5 t., 3 s. 14th r. 6 s., 9 t., 2 ch., 3 t. with 2 ch., in between into the same space ; 3 ch., 3 t. with 2 ch. in between into the same space ; 1 s., 9 t., 5 s. 15th r. 5 s., 5 t., 1 s., 5 t., 1 s., 5 t., 1 s., 5 t., 1 s., 5 t. 5 s. 16th r. 6 s., 9 t., 1 s., 9 t., 1 s., 9 t., 5 s. 17th r. 6 s., 5 t., 1 s., 5 t., 1 s., 5 t., 1 s., 5 t., 6 s. 18th r. 10 s., 9 t., 9 s. 19th r. 10 s., 5 t., 10 s. 20th r. 22 s. 21st r. 22s. The medallions can be repeated to form insertion or joined to form a bag.

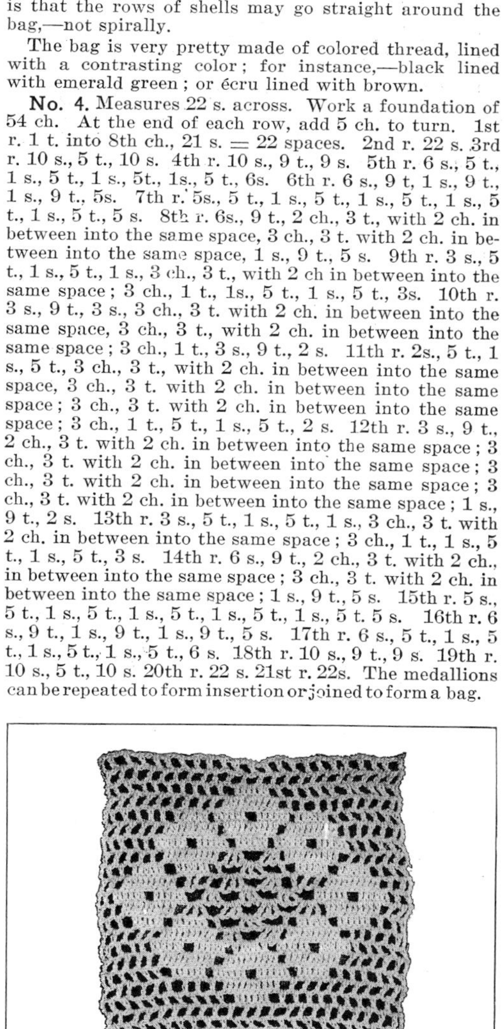

No. 4

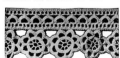

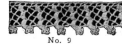

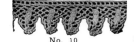

EASY SMOCKING FOR CHILDREN'S CLOTHES*

By HELENA BUEHLER

A REVIVAL of smocking, which has long been one of the most popular forms of trimming used by English mothers for their children's clothes, is now apparent in the newest children's dresses displayed in our leading stores.

While the method of this stitch is simple, the new worker will require some guidance by the experienced, and the amateur will need quite a little practice to insure good results.

As a method of trimming children's clothes, young girls' garments, ladies' waists and négligées of soft material—in fact, wherever fullness is desired—this form of needlework is especially adapted.

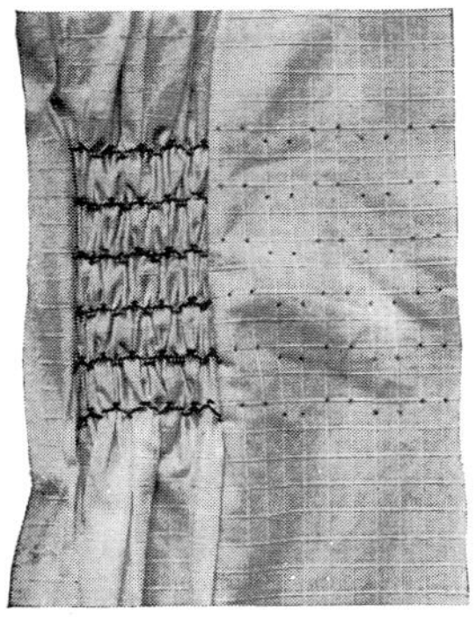

Another practical advantage lies in the fact that the fullness made by smocking allows for the growth of the child, and many a garment that otherwise might have to be discarded may be made to last another season by the simple act of letting out tucks or a hem to give length. These dresses, though trim, allow perfect freedom of motion and are graceful as well as youthful.

Figure IV—Sampler 2

The softer wash fabrics (which do not muss readily) such as gingham, shirting, Madras, a corded crêpe (narrow stripes, ⅛ to ⅜ inches apart), checks and crossbars are especially good materials to use for smocking. The stripes and crossbars serve as guides to keep the smocking straight and even.

Smocking is an ideal trimming for dresses of cashmere, challis, albatross or other soft woolen material. As there are no stripes and crossbars for guides in these plain materials, transfer patterns may be used or the lines and dots may be marked with chalk on dark goods and with pencil on light goods, for the effect depends largely upon the evenness of the stitch. Figure I illustrates the method of marking plain goods for the combination of stitches shown in Figure VIIa.

Figure II—Sampler 1   Figure III

A dainty design may be developed by the use of pink or pale-blue thread on a white dimity or crossbarred muslin. A touch of red or dark blue is charming on a white-striped or corded Madras. A checked or striped material is attractive with the stitch done in cotton of the same shade that appears in the goods, while white stitches are always in good taste.

Before attempting to trim a dress the novice should practice on a sampler, such as is shown in Fig. II in single cable-stitch. To make this sampler, place a strip of colored gingham with a white stripe on a flat surface, and two inches below the top of the goods on the right side rule a line with tailor's chalk in some contrasting color which can be readily seen. Directly under this line rule three others each one inch below the one above. Then thread an ordinary sewing needle, size 1 or 2, with crochet cotton No. 10 or No. 5. Knot one end of the moderately long thread. Bring the needle through on the ruled line across the first narrow white stripe, No. 1, at the left-hand side of material, keeping the knot on the under side of the material; then proceed to the next stripe, No. 2, putting the needle under the stripe and at right angles to it—that is, pointed straight across toward the left hand. Keeping the thread below the needle, pull gently toward the first stitch and hold in place with thumb and first finger of the left hand while you proceed to the next stripe, No. 3, putting the needle in and under the narrow stripe (pointed toward the left just as you did for the first stitch, but this time keep the thread above the needle and pull toward the last stitch).

Always insert the needle on the ruled line and under the stripe pointing in the same direction (from right to left) but keeping the thread just below, then just above, the line until the stitch is drawn into its place—that is, 1st stitch, keep thread below needle; 2d stitch, thread above needle; 3d stitch, thread below; 4th

*Copyright 1914 by The Curtis Publishing Company

stitch, thread above, and so on to the end of line. After a little practice it is comparatively easy to keep all of the stitches straight and even. The lines below are a repetition of this work. After you have finished all of the rows hold the material with the left hand and with the right hand gently pull the fullness in place as you would for gathers. In this sampler only the first, simplest stitch is used. The effect may be varied by different spacing, as is shown in Fig. III.

Sampler No. 2. This second sampler shows a slightly more complicated stitch in points, which is, however, very easily done. It is one-half row of diamond stitch. For this model a strip of white crossbarred muslin is used and pencil dots take the place of the ruled guide lines. Place the first dot at an intersection of the bars on a horizontal bar about two inches from the top. Make dot 2 on this same line at the next intersection. Dot 3 is made on the next vertical bar, but ⅛ inch below the horizontal bar, and dot 4 on the next line is also ⅛ inch below. For the next two dots go up to the horizontal bar again, and for the next two come down ⅛ inch again, and so on across the sampler. For the second row of stitching begin two spaces below the first horizontal bar and dot as you did for the first row. Space four more rows in the same way. See Fig. IV.

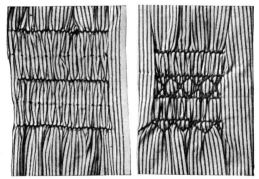

Figure VIa   Figure VIb

Begin just as you did in Sampler No. 1, at the left-hand corner and on the top line, leaving the knot on the wrong side of the material. Insert the needle through dot 1 and then pass under dot 2 (pointing the needle from right to left, straight across the material on the bar). Keep the thread above the needle while dot 2 is drawn toward dot 1 and is held in position with the thumb and first finger of the left hand, and next pass the needle under dot 3, again keeping the thread above while you pull dot 3 gently back. Now pass the needle under dot 4, but this time keep the thread below the needle; pull back and proceed to dot 5, keeping the thread below the needle while you pull the stitch into place.

Always put the needle in straight across the material and pointed from right to left. You will notice that to form this stitch you keep the thread first above the needle for two consecutive stitches and so on until you finish the row. Repeat this method for the next five rows.

Sampler No. 3 is shown in complete diamond stitch. It is really an elaboration of No. 2, since its block design is made by two rows in one of which the points are up and in the other they are down. Again use a strip of crossbarred Madras, beginning as before on a horizontal bar about two inches from the top. However, instead of putting the first two dots on this bar place them just below in order to allow room for the upper points. As before place the third and fourth dots ⅜

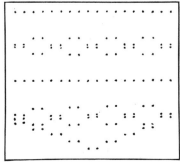

Figure I

inch below the horizontal bar, etc., as shown in the illustration. Just above the horizontal bar and over dots 1 and 2 place two dots on which you begin the upper points. Place dots 3 and 4 of this row on the same vertical line as for the corresponding dots on the lower row, but this time ⅜ inch above the horizontal bar. Complete the row as shown in Fig V. Five rows of these diamonds should be about an inch apart. For the actual work first do the upper points as you did in Sampler 2. Next work the row above the horizontal

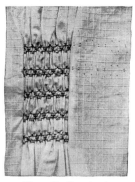

Figure V—Sampler 3   Figure VIIc

line, but in this case reverse the order of holding the thread—that is, in making first two stitches keep the thread below the needle, for next two stitches hold it above, etc. Larger diamonds are formed by working down, 3, 4 or 5 stitches (just as we have worked two in this sampler), then up 3, 4 or 5, etc., etc.

Fig. VI, a, b, shows variations and combinations of the stitches used in making the three samplers. The simplest of these is found in a, in which in the second and fourth rows the fullness is held in place at intervals by two back stitches, giving the effect of embroidered dots. In b you will find a combination cable, point and diamond-stitch, 1, 2 and 3. Four rows are worked 1 inch apart in the first stitch. Between rows 2 and 3 the diamond design is carried out in five-stitch points. Below the last row is a single five-point row.

In Fig. VII, a, b and c, are shown four rows in other attractive though somewhat more complicated variations of the three stitches, which are, however, also easy to do.

Any of these designs or other original variations may be applied to dresses or other garments, and it is easily seen that with different materials and threads of different colors an almost endless variety may be obtained. One may use smocking as the sole trimming for a child's wardrobe and still express originality in each garment.

If a Bishop style of dress is chosen (as pattern No. 8551), make the frock with the exception of putting on the neck-band and finish the sleeves simply with a narrow hem, for a narrow band for smocking forms the little cuff. Now mark your dress for the smocking, making the first line 1½ or 2 inches from neck. You can vary the distance of rows from each other according to your wish; viz., copy Sampler No. 1, making lines only ¾ or ½ inch apart.

After all the smocking is finished gather the neck-line to suit the size of the neck band. A small, round, turn-over collar finished with a featherstitched hem is best adapted to this style of dress, as it relieves the plainness of the upper unsmocked material. When using patterns similar to that used in the Devonshire smocked dress the material is smocked before the dress is cut out.

For holding in fullness at the waist and sleeves of a little boy's jacket or rompers smocking is ideal.

A word about the laundering of the smocked garments may not go amiss here: The smocking should not be rubbed on a board, and if ironed at all should be ironed on the wrong side.

The stripes are ¼ inch apart in Sample No. 1, but stripes 1-16, ⅛, ¼ and ⅜ inch apart are adaptable for a guide. If finer stripes than ¼ inch apart are used, every second or third stripe is taken for a stitch instead of every stripe.

Tailor's chalk may be purchased at department stores for one cent each or ten cents a dozen, assorted colors. It is easily rubbed off after the work is finished.

Clark's crochet cotton, No. 5 or No. 10 (10 cents a ball); D. M. C. crochet cotton No. 8 or No. 10. When smocking finer fabrics, dimity or batiste, a finer thread, about No. 20, should be used.

Transfer patterns Nos. 12960, Vandyke smocking, and 12961, band-smocking, may be had for 10 cents each. These serve as a guide where plain materials are used.

Figure VIIa   Figure VIIb

14055—Silk cording is smart on suits and dresses. ¾ and 1¼ inches wide, 3 yards of each in the pattern. 10 cents

14142—In cord and embroidered dots on net. 1¾ inches wide, 3 yards. 10 cents

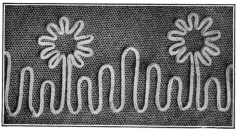

14270—Developed in very fine soutache on net. 2½ inches wide, 3 yards. 10 cents

14596—Developed in two shades of blue and gold on net. 2¼ yards, 4¼ inches wide. 15 cents

14240—Soutache braiding on net. ¾ and 1½ inches wide respectively, 3 yards of each. 10 cents

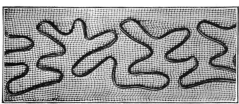

14272—Developed on square mesh net in heavy soutache. 3 inches wide, 3 yards. 15 cents

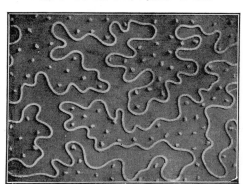

14496—Carried out in rat-tail cord and French dots on charmeuse. 7 inches wide, 1½ yards in the pattern. 15 cents

14533—For underwear and children's clothes. 6½ inches wide, 1½ yards. 15 cents

14319—For braid and solid work. 3¾ inches wide, 2 yards. 10 cents

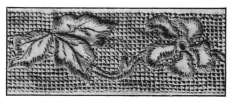

14490—For punched work or darning. 2½ inches wide, 3 yards. 10 cents

14522—A beautiful border for the lingerie dress. 7½ inches wide, 1½ yards. 15 cents

14505—For solid and evelet work. 5½ inches wide, 2¼ yards. 15 cents

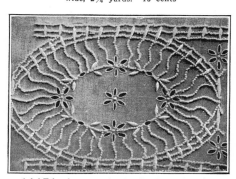

14471—An attractive border for a lingerie dress. 7½ inches wide, 3 yards. 15 cents

14364—Developed by couching heavy wool with silk on marquisette. 1-inch wide, 6 yards and 4 corners. 10 cents.

14278—Developed in flat braid on serge. ¾ and 1½ inches wide, 3 yards of each width. 10 cents.

14570—Conventional border for embroidering dresses of cotton, linen or silk material. 2 inches wide. 3 yards. 10 cents.

14181—For embroidering waists and dresses of net and silk, 3¼ inches wide, 2 yards. 10 cents.

14147—In cord, solid work and beads. Suitable for embroidering wool or silk materials. 2 inches wide, 3 yards. 10 cents.

14483—Developed in coronation cord. ¾-inch wide, 6 yards and 4 corners. 10 cents.

14244—Carried out in soutache and French dots on crepe de Chine. 2½ inches wide, 3 yards. 10 cents

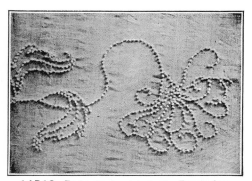

14519—To be developed in beads, French dots or outline-stitch. 5 inches wide, 1½ yards. 10 cents

DAINTY DESIGNS FOR EMBROIDERING COLLARS

14683

14668

14658

14683—Rose design for collar and two motifs. This attractive design should be embroidered on very fine lawn, batiste or handkerchief linen. The edge of the flowers should be developed in buttonhole-stitch, and the leaves embroidered in solid work, or outline and seed stitch. The motifs may be used on cuffs, vests, or tie-ends. 15 cents.

14670—Design for embroidering a shirt-waist. Pattern includes collar, cuffs, revers, and tabs. This design is appropriate for embroidering waists, of linen, lawn, or crêpe de Chine. To be developed in white, in solid work and eyelets, using mercerized cotton for wash materials and filo silk for crêpe de Chine. It is illustrated on waist pattern 7967. 15 cents each.

14658—Design for Medici collar and revers. Pattern includes sailor collar, standing collar, and revers. This design should be stamped on handkerchief linen, lawn or batiste, and the standing portion should be wired with invisible collar stays, or fine milliners' wire. Solid work and eyelets combined may be used in carrying out this design in white or colors. 10 cents.

14668—Three designs for embroidering collars. Two Japanese designs may be embroidered in colors on linen, ratine or the material of the blouse or frock. The third design should be embroidered in white, in solid work and eyelets, on fine lawn, batiste, or handkerchief linen. This collar may be wired and worn standing, if desired. 15 cents.

14409—Sailor collar and cuffs. May be embroidered in solid work or eyelets on handkerchief or round-thread linen. This set is especially appropriate for a young girls' dress of serge or ratine. 15 cents.

14670   14668

14501—Sailor collar in punched work. This makes an exceptionally pretty collar for wear with a suit-coat or dress. It should be worked on loosely woven linen. 15 cents.

14403—Coat Set. May be embroidered in colors to match the suit with which it is to be worn. 15 cents.

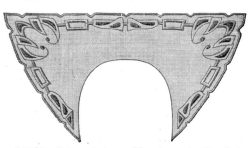

14640—Collar design. May be embroidered in several bright colors or two or more shades of one color. It should be worked in solid work and outline stitch on handkerchief linen, lawn or batiste. This pattern also includes motifs which may be used on cuffs or sash-ends. 10 cents.

14242—Round collar and cuffs. This dainty design in solid work should be stamped on handkerchief linen. 15 cents.

HOW TO MAKE THE NEW BASQUE DRESS

By FLORENCE BURCHARD

THE new Basque, with its long, easy fitting lines, is hardly to be compared with the old-time garment of that name, narrow in back and pulled in like an hour-glass at the waistline. It is a general favorite just now and is youthful and becoming.

The Basque dress shown here is for a young girl or small woman. It opens down the front and consists of a gathered guimpe, a two-piece skirt with two deep, straight flounces and an outside Basque.

How to Cut

If the woman who makes her own dresses will follow the directions given with the pattern she is using there is no reason for failure.

All perforations must be followed explicitly. In cutting, lay the pieces showing the two large holes on the straight of the goods; those showing one large hole on a lengthwise fold. Mark perforations indicating gathers, folds or plaits with tailor's tacks in a thread that shows up well on the material.

The Guimpe

Lay pattern on material as directed and cut, taking care to indicate all notches. Baste pieces together, notches matching; try on and make the required alterations. If this guimpe or underwaist is made of net or thin material, under-arms and shoulder may be finished with French seams. This finish cannot be used with the armholes to any advantage; it is better to set in the sleeves in the usual way and bind the seam edges with silk binding or else turn them in carefully and overcast them.

The bottom of this gathered underwaist is set into a narrow belt which may be of the material or of muslin. To adjust the belt, put the garment on and draw a tape tightly around the waistline; raise your arms slightly until the waist fits easily; arrange the gathers and pin them into place on the tape. Gather the waist along this line and cut off any extra material. The belt may be seamed on by machine, then turned and felled down on the wrong side by hand. Snap fasteners may be used to close it. It has been found very prac-

View Four
The Inside

View Three
The Lining

View Two
The Flounce

View One
The Guimpe

8612

tical also to use them to fasten guimpe and skirt together; this prevents the guimpe from working up from the waistline. Sew the sockets about an inch apart on the outside of the narrow belt as illustrated in No. 1, and the balls at corresponding distances on the inside belt of the skirt.

The Skirt

This is a two-piece skirt gathered slightly at the top. The hang of the skirt depends almost entirely upon the way the material is cut, so be very careful to see that the two large holes are on the straight of the material before taking up the scissors.

Baste the side seams of the skirt at the seam allowance, notches matching; stitch, taking care not to have the tension too tight, if you sew them by machine, or the seams will draw. If a transparent material such as net or lace is used the seam edges should be turned in and overcast by hand; if silk or satin, the seams should be pressed open and the edges bound with seam binding.

Finish the placket by making an underlap of the material about an inch and a half wide; with thin material this should be made double, but on heavier stuff it is better to bind the edges of a single thickness.

Slip this underlap neatly under the left edge of the placket and stitch into place; the right edge should be faced. Arrange patent fasteners along the placket about an inch apart.

The Inside Belt

The inside belt may be made of silk or cotton belting about two or two and a half inches wide or of a piece of cambric; it is fitted slightly by darts arranged on either side; these are indicated on the pattern. Finish this belt with hooks and eyes down the front and baste the skirt onto it, having the ends of the belt at the placket edges and allowing the skirt to extend about a quarter to a half an inch above the belt. Try the skirt on and if properly adjusted turn a quarter of an inch allowance over the belt and stitch with short, firm, hand stitches; cover this raw edge with seam binding sewed on flat. Try the skirt on again and turn up the hem; this is not difficult to do oneself, standing before a mirror; when you are quite sure that the skirt is even all around turn the hem in at the top and sew by hand.

The Flounces

It is a simple matter to adjust these straight flounces; in this instance they are of lace and no finish is required at the bottom. An effective way of finishing such flounces at the bottom when they are made of soft silk, satin or taffetas, is to turn up a hem of about an inch or an inch and a half on the right side and slip or blind-stitch it down.

As shown in No. 2, the flounces are shirred over a cord a trifle thinner than an ordinary lead pencil; another attractive way would be to cover the cord with the material of the Basque, taffetas, satin or whatever it happened to be, and gather the flounce on to it, thus forming a heading.

The Basque

A dart-fitted foundation or lining is used in the Basque; it may be of thin cambric, mull or silk. Quite as much attention should be given to the cutting of the lining as the outside and the perforations and notches noted as carefully.

Baste the lining on the right side and try on; pin it together with the fronts meeting. This lining should fit easily and not draw. When all necessary changes have been noted, turn the lining and baste on the wrong

View Six
Inside Finish

View Five
The Outside and
Girdle Adjusted

side; slash open the darts and stretch them ever so gently along each edge; this should also be done with the fronts. Try on again and if perfect the darts and center back seams may be stitched, shoulders and underarms being left open so that the outsides can be sewn in with them.

Turn in the front edges of the lining the width allowed and stitch about a quarter of an inch from the fold, allowing the edges to remain open; sew the hooks and eyes on about an inch apart, hooks and eyes alternating down the fronts. The eyes should be allowed to project enough to hook well and the hooks be set in slightly so that the fronts will not gap. The free edges of the hems may now be turned back and hemmed down neatly over the bases of the hooks and eyes. Finish the seams of the lining by overcasting the edges or binding them.

Adjusting the Outside of the Basque

Pin the outside and the lining together at shoulder and underarms seams with notches matching and baste. It is also better to catch the outside of the lining together at the top and around the armholes with a line of basting. Stitch shoulder and underarm seams, press open and bind. Turn the edges of the armholes in and slash wherever necessary so that they will lie flat; seam binding should be used to cover these slashed edges or a bias strip of the material about a half an inch in width, sewn on neatly by hand. Turn in the top of the outside and the lining facing each other, the width allowed, allowing the outside to extend a little above the lining so as to cover it and hem by hand on the wrong side. The fronts are turned in and hemmed very carefully by hand, care being taken that the stitches do not show.

The bottom of the Basque, lining and outside together, is turned up and hemmed by hand. In order to preserve the straight outline of the Basque a line of weights, which may be purchased by the yard, is run through the hem all around the bottom of the garment, catching them here and there to prevent them from slipping out of place. A narrow bias binding is used to finish the slashes through which the sash is passed.

Buttonholes

Buttonholes may be worked in the usual way or they may be bound. Perhaps the easiest thing to do is to sew the buttons to the right side of the Basque and close it with snap fasteners set on the inside about an inch and a half apart.

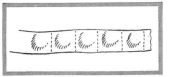

Lead-weighted Tape

BASQUE WAISTS AND OVERBLOUSES

8285—Ladies' and misses' vest waist. Full-length sleeves with flare cuff, or elbow sleeves. Cuts in sizes 32 to 42 inches bust measure and requires in size 36 for the underwaist 1½ yards of 36-inch material, with ¾ yard of 32-inch or wider material for vest. Price 15 cents.

8357—Ladies' and misses' raglan waist. Full-length sleeves perforated for shorter length; patch pocket and high turn down or round collar. Pattern cuts in sizes 34 to 46 inches bust measure and will require for size 36, 2¼ yards of 36-inch material. Price of pattern 15 cents.

8555—Ladies' and misses' Basque waist, with sailor or Directoire collar and with two styles of sleeves, a full-length dart-fitted sleeve and a tucked sleeve. The pattern cuts in sizes 32 to 44 inches bust measure and requires in size 36, 2⅛ yards of 36-inch material. Price 15 cents.

8562—Ladies' and misses' Basque waist, a kimono guimpe opening in front and a Basque overblouse closing in back. Cuts in sizes 32 to 42 inches bust measure and size 36 requires 2¼ yards of 36-inch material and 1¼ yards of 36-inch material for the overblouse. Price 15 cents.

8569—Ladies' and misses' peplum blouse with full-length sleeve, with a pointed circular cuff, and a plaited or pointed collar. Peplum cut in straight or square tab outline. Pattern cuts in sizes 32 to 46 inches bust measure, requiring for size 36, 2½ yards of 36-inch material. Price 15 cents.

8555

8569

8562

8285

8357

8592–8568—Ladies' and misses' Basque combined with ladies' three-piece tunic skirt. The Basque opens in front and has full-length sleeves with turn back cuffs and large Directoire collar. The front extends into a sash. The skirt has slightly raised waistline and a three-piece narrow tunic, the tunic to be cut plain or in square tab outline. Pattern for the Basque cuts in sizes 32 to 42 inches bust measure and the skirt in sizes 22 to 32 inches waist measure. The dress, as illustrated, requires in size 36, 3¾ yards of 36-inch plain material and 3 yards striped material, and 1⅞ yards 36-inch lining. Price of patterns 15 cents each.

LATEST DESIGNS IN SEPARATE SKIRTS

8528—Ladies' three-piece, gathered skirt, with slightly raised waistline and four gathered flounces, and with or without gathered yoke. Pattern cuts in size 22 to 32 inches waist measure, and requires for size 24, 5⅞ yards of 36-inch material, with ⅞ yard of 27-inch lining. Price of pattern 15 cents.

8532—Ladies' three-piece skirt with s l i g h t l y raised waistline, and shaped inset sections in godet effect. Skirt is cut 1½ inches above regular waistline. Pattern cuts in sizes 22 to 34 inches waist measure, requiring for size 24, 3¾ yards of 36-inch material. Price of pattern 15 cents.

8575—Ladies' three-piece normal waistline skirt with one-piece accordion plaited, or gathered tunic. Cuts in sizes 22 to 32 inches waist measure. In size 24 it will require 3¼ yards of 36-inch net, with 2¼ yards of 30-inch material for underskirt. Price of pattern 15 cents.

8587—Ladies' s k i r t. Three-piece foundation, lengthened by a straight, one-piece flounce with a two-piece tunic. Pattern cuts in sizes 22 to 32-inch waist measure, requiring for size 24, 2⅝ yards of 36-inch material, with 1⅝ yards 15-inch contrasting material cut on cross-wise fold. Price 15 cents.

8591—Ladies' one-piece straight-gathered skirt, opening in the back. The trimming bands give body to the skirt and hold it out in the full effect which is so fashionable. The pattern cuts in sizes 22 to 32-inch waist measure, and will require for size 24, 4 yards of 36-inch material. Price 15 cents.

8381-8524—Thoroughly American is this combination of a plain shirt-waist and plaited skirt. The waist has a high turn-down collar, or V-neck and shaped collars and full-length shirt sleeve perforated for elbow length. Pattern cuts for ladies and misses in sizes 32 to 50 inches bust measure, requiring for size 36, 2¼ yards of 36-inch material. Ladies' straight plaited skirt, No. 8524, may be made with or without four-piece yoke. Pattern cuts in sizes 22 to 32 inches waist measure, requiring for size 24, 5½ yards of 36-inch material. Price 15 cents each.

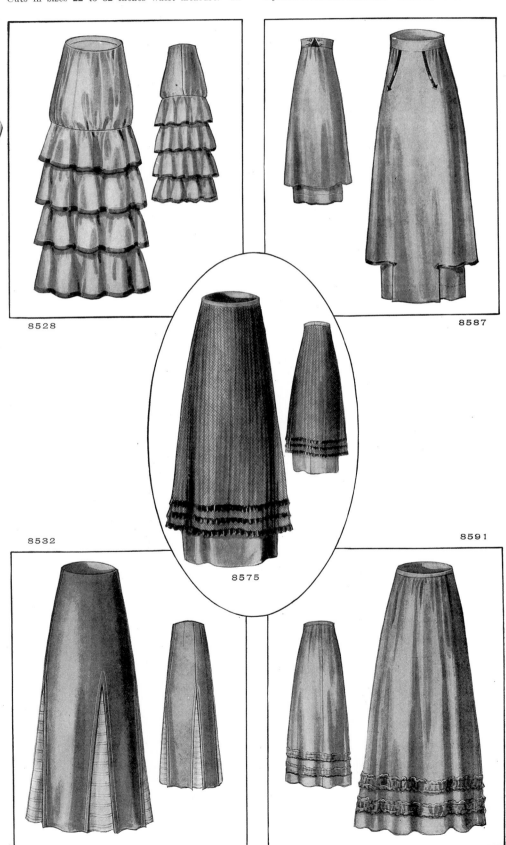

8528

8587

8532

8575

8591

COMFY COLD WEATHER BATH-ROBES
NEW LINGERIE WITH SIMPLE LINES

8149—Fleecy blankets with their classic borders make the most comfortable bath-robes for winter wear and a pattern particularly suited to cutting out such a garment is No. 8149. The pattern cuts in sizes 32, 36, 40 and 44 inches bust measure and will require a blanket 72 inches wide and 90 inches long, in any size. Pattern 15 cents.

8602-8621—Embroidered flouncing makes the most attractive corset cover, cut from pattern 8602, which includes a peplum, and sleeve shields. A five-gored petticoat is shown with this. Pattern 8602 cuts in sizes 32, 36, 40, 44 and 48 inches bust measure, requiring in size 36, 2⅜ yards 15-inch embroidered flouncing. Skirt pattern cuts in sizes 22 to 34 inches waist measure, requiring in size 24, 4⅛ yards 36-inch material with 2½ yards 12-inch flouncing and 1⅜ yards quilling. Patterns 10 and 15 cents.

7267-14271—The most popular nightgown is the one-piece model. It developes well in sheer material with bits of embroidery. For this purpose transfer No. 14271 is good (containing a design for nightgown, chemise or corset-cover and costing 15 cents).

Pattern for nightgown is cut in size 32, 36, 40 and 44 inches bust measure, requiring in size 36, 3¾ yards 36-inch material. Pattern 15 cents.

8598 is a simple négligée with full-length sleeves and large pockets particularly adapted to sleeping car or state-room, providing a thorough cover-all for the figure and room in its pockets for toilette articles. It cuts in bishop style, requiring for size 36, 6¾ yards of 36-inch material. Pattern cuts in sizes 32, 36, 40, 44 and 48 inches bust measure. Pattern 15 cents.

8620-8105-14606—A simple pattern containing a simple and practical kimono to be made in two ways is 8620. This is trimmed with transfer pattern 14606 (3 Bulgarian borders. 3 yards and 4 corners of each. Price 10 cents). With this is shown a two-piece petticoat with slightly gathered flounce. Kimono pattern cuts in sizes 34 to 44 inches, requiring in size 36, 3½ yards 30-inch material with ⅝ yard contrasting goods, and the skirt pattern in sizes 22 to 34 inches waist measure, requiring in sizes 24, 2½ yards 42-inch material. Patterns 15 cents each.

8598

8620-8105
Emb. 14606

8598   8620-8105

8149   8602-8621   7267

8602-8621

8149

7267
Emb. 14271

CORSETS FOLLOW FASHION'S LEAD

By KATE RAFTER

FOR several seasons past the corset manufacturers have been bringing forward every device to provide a corset that suits the natural figure; molding, rather than boning, is the order of the day. Steels are few and far between, and materials especially woven to take their place in part or whole are largely used in their manufacture, under different trade names, such as "The Grecian-Trico," "Lastikops" and "Goowinette." They all tend to confine proportions that are unduly prominent and by gentle pressure and elasticity reduce the figure. Although these materials give great

quite as pliable for parts that require elasticity. The bust gores of this material, for instance, are finished in such a manner that they may be adjusted to suit the figure.

Corset B is one of the front-lacing models. So many women like this style. The elastic intersections and the hose-supporter, which is non-elastic, are new features of the Birdsey-Somers corset, known as the Elso.

The corset marked C is an ultrastylish model for medium and slender figures; the bust-gores running

B

G   A   F

D

satisfaction, it must not be thought that the reliable coutil and handsome broches, combined with boning and fine steels, are going out, or even the especially woven elastic used in parts requiring pliability; all these are still in use. Corsets are very surely, although slowly, assuming a little more curve and slightly higher bust support, to follow the dictates of fashion.

Never in the history of corset-making has "health, comfort and style" been so scientifically considered as to-day. Beauty of line, common sense in construction and comfort in wear are so thorough, a woman no longer has the need to take off her corsets to be comfortable. She can wear them while attending to the duties of her household and with equal comfort enjoy a seat in the orchestra of a theater.

One of the most notable manufacturers has a correspondence school in connection with its establishment, teaching saleswomen how to sell and how to judge of the requirements of a customer, just as other firms send demonstrators to show how to put on a corset and adjust the supporters.

The corset marked A is known as the Trico-Vee, one of the Bien Jolie models. The makers are the inventors of the Grecian-Trico weave, a material introduced in place of elastic as being more durable, and

to far below the waistline give ample breathing space, while the Steel-tex batiste of which it is constructed makes it very durable. It has world-wide fame under the trade name of Nemo.

The well-known R. & G. corset is pictured in D. This illustrates one of the many styles put on the market each season. It conforms to the newest line of fashion, and has all the necessary qualities that go to the making of a perfect corset.

One of the Gossard models is illustrated in E. The front lacing is a special feature of this firm's output. The proportions of this artistic corset conform to the natural figure, while they follow the latest dictates of fashion. It is made of a beautiful mercerized grenadine brocade.

The Goodwin corset, designed by a woman of artistic and scientific ability, is shown in drawing F. The lines give erectness of form and the pliability of the woven material make it an ideal corset for the dance.

The illustration marked G is one of the very newest W. B. models. A corset of such renown leaves very little to tell. It is, however, noteworthy of the makers of this corset that they excel in fit, construction, durability and appearance. Their selection gives a "Fit for every figure, a price for every purse."

C

E

NÉGLIGÉES AND UNDERWEAR
FOR THE WINTER WARDROBE

8617–8428

8604

8071

8604
Emb. 14465

8617–8428

8071

7958—Pajamas for women and girls may seem to be somewhat of a departure from the established custom, but many women find comfort in them. The pattern is cut with standing or round collar, or it may be made collarless. The full-length sleeves are perforated for elbow length. The pattern comes in sizes 28, 32, 36 and 40 inches bust measure, size 36 requiring 6½ yards of 27-inch material. Price 15 cents.

8617–8428—This négligée is made of chiffon, but it would be more practical made in batiste or handkerchief linen. It is worn with a three-piece petticoat that may be made with plaited, circular or gathered flounces. The pattern for the négligée comes in sizes 32, 36, 40 and 44 inches bust measure, while the petticoat comes in sizes 22 to 38 inches waist measure. You will require for the négligée in size 36, 2¼ yards 36-inch material and the skirt in size 24 takes 4 yards 36-inch material. Price of patterns 15 cents each.

8604–14465—Home-made underwear is considered far superior to ready-made and it is very easy to make if a good pattern is used. This combination corset-cover and closed drawers which is cut for ladies and misses is an excellent one. It comes in sizes 32 to 44 inches bust measure, requiring for size 36, 3¼ yards 30-inch material. The dainty embroidery used on this combination may be done in eyelet and outline work and it is 1 inch wide, 6 yards and 4 corners in the pattern. Price 10 cents. Combination pattern price 15 cents.

8071—Many interesting designs in eiderdown and quilted silks are shown in the shops which are excellent for making up a kimono such as pattern 8071. It is cut in short sweep, perforated for round length and dressing sacque length, and has two styles of collars. It cuts in sizes 32 to 48 inches bust measure, requiring in size 36, 4¾ yards 36-inch material, with ¾ yard 36-inch contrasting goods. Price 15 cents.

8408—An undergarment quite necessary for the new dance frocks is No. 8408. It has low round neck, perforated for low bust line, and may be made with plaited or gathered ruffle. It should be embroidered with pattern No. 14515 which is 2¼ inches wide and has 3 yards in the pattern. Price 10 cents. The slip cuts in sizes 32 to 46 inches bust measure, requiring for size 36, 3 yards 36-inch material. Price 15 cents.

7958

8408

QUAINT NOVELTIES IN DESIGN MARK THE NEW SILKS

A SOFT green printed surah silk is shown in the upper center of the page with a formal design in Russian colorings.

T HE material in the center is copied directly from the wonderful ceiling that Paul Hellieu designed for the Grand Central station.

S HOWN above is a checkerboard of black and white, broken up by conventionalized designs in contrasting but subdued colorings. The material is soft-finished crêpe de Chine.

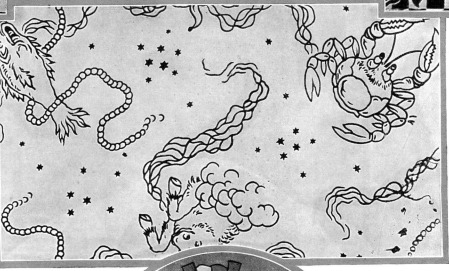

T HE navy and white checkboard taffeta illustrated above is relieved by stiff American beauty roses and foliage in the natural colors and is used effectively for trimmings.

B UTTERFLIES in natural shades flutter lazily over the chiffon below, from which wonderful evening gowns may be fashioned.

S TRIPES which were so popular in the spring have now taken on dizzy undulations and many new colors which are giving them fresh life.

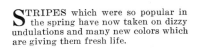

C HIFFONS and metal tissues printed with weird Aztec and Egyptian figures are effective, on just the right person, but like all extreme novelties should be used with discretion.

CAREFUL CONSIDERATION OF THE STOUT WOMAN'S NEEDS

THERE seems to be no other phase of women's costuming which is so little understood as that of the stout woman's problem. Most other women can be guided by their personal likes and dislikes, and while occasionally they will be anxious to wear unbecoming colors, still these can be minimized by careful selection of accessories, but in the stout woman's case this is different. In the first place, she usually likes bright, "happy" colors; she is fond of "cheerful" figured materials and generally feels that the small hat makes her inconspicuous, and these are the three pitfalls it is most important she should escape. If she goes in for the lighter colors at all, they should be in subtle combinations of the half-tone shades. She should never use the primary colors. As to figures, she should eschew almost all but the invisible stripes, as she should the high surface satins and velvets. Then, in the matter of hats, she should consider that a tiny one throws her entire figure into prominence, as a tight skirt would, whereas, if she has an ample skirt and good sized hats, her shoulders, bust and hips are thrown into comparative insignificance.

Next in importance is the consideration of line, and this is very important. Most stout women are fond of having what fullness there is, drawn into a tight fan at the waist, which is a fatal mistake. Instead, these lines should be distributed evenly across the figure as this breaks up the space into a number of small spaces, instead of two broad expanses at the sides and a small bunch of fullness at the center. Most stout women have felt that kimono sleeves are unbecoming, but this is not always so, for when the bust is large it is best not to accentuate the arm line, which in many cases makes the shoulders look small and the bust large. The two latter points are well illustrated by the dress on the middle of the page, No. 8523. In this dress the long trimming lines break the figure into almost equal sections, and the loose blouse, with its low drooping shoulder-line, makes the bust look comparatively small. If

this dress is to be made up by a stout woman who is also short, the contrasting skirt facing had best be omitted. The pattern for this dress cuts in sizes 34 to 44 inches bust measure, and in size 40 you will require 5 yards 42-inch material, with 2¾ yards 36-inch contrasting material for hem facings, girdle and trimming bands, 1 yard 36-inch net and 2 yards 36-inch lining. Pattern 15 cents.

Another dress particularly good for stout women is illustrated in Nos. 8527-8601. It is illustrated in a lustrous brown cashmere with the vest of striped silk. The long, pointed vests tend to give a slim appearance to the figure and the slightly gathered, three-piece skirt is both comfortable and good-looking. The waist pat-

8523   8527-8601

tern cuts in sizes 34 to 46 inches bust measure and the skirt in sizes 22 to 32 inches waist measure. For the dress in sizes 42-30, you will require 6⅞ yards 36-inch material, with ¾ yard 27-inch contrasting material. Patterns 15 cents each.

In Nos. 8605-8616, still another good combination is illustrated. Here a Basque waist with a girdle at the sides and back and an inset chemisette is combined with a plaited skirt, whose yoke and front panels are cut in one. The simple style of the Basque and the center-front closing of waist and skirt are good features for the stout woman, while the plaited skirt is always excellent for her. The blouse pattern cuts in sizes 32 to 42 inches bust measure and the skirt in sizes 22 to 34 inches waist measure. In sizes 40-28, you will require 7¾ yards 36-inch material, with ¾ yard 36-inch contrasting material for chemisette. Patterns 15 cents each.

The military styles which are so popular this season are excellent for the stout woman with their somewhat severe lines and flat braidings, but, of course, when a woman finds herself stout, she should stop using the latest styles and instead spend many hours before her mirror to find just what lines and colors suit her best. Then she should stick to these through thick and thin, making only such changes in her clothes as will keep them up-to-date. Like the extremely homely woman, she should make every effort to have her disposition and conversation so pleasing and interesting that what she wears becomes of minor importance.

Many women feel that because they are large they should wear tight-fitting clothes, but this is another error. Cross-lines are bad on the stout figure and if the clothes are snug these cross-lines are very likely to appear, whereas if the clothes are cut quite loose and roomy, they will hang in natural and graceful lines.

On page 6 you will find another short article on the stout woman's needs, and by running through the book you will see a number of excellent designs, as, for instance, 8640 on page 3, 8635 on page 4, 8561 on page 13, 8379-8568-8579 on page 18, 8615-8618 on page 19, 8525-8524 on page 53 and many others through the book. Should any personal problems arise in connection with the use of our patterns for stout figures, we shall be very glad to answer correspondence, if you will state fully and clearly just what the problem is.

8605-8616

8523

FULLNESS IS THE KEYNOTE FOR SKIRTS
WHILE BIBS AND BASQUES ARE POPULAR

8566

8555-8556

8582

8566   8555-8556   8582

8566—Now that the season for winter evening clothes is here, the subject takes on new interest. While we are told that sewed-in sleeves are "the newest thing" the body-and-sleeve-in-one feature seems to be as popular for evening clothes, and No. 8566, illustrated above, has a kimono blouse over which is worn a gathered bib with shaped trimming pieces extending toward the shoulders. The skirt is a three-piece model with a gathered ruffle in tunic effect and a draped sash. This will develop well in a combination of Nile green taffetas and cream colored point d'Esprit and a large American Beauty rose would add to the effect. The pattern cuts in sizes 34 to 42 inches bust measure and will require in size 36, 3¾ yards 36-inch satin, with 3⅝ yards 27-inch net for blouse, sleeve ruffles and skirt flounce. Pattern 15 cents.

8555-8556—A new note is given to the late fashions by the full tucked skirts which are part of many of the smartest models. Cut on the straight of the goods, they measure between two and three yards around the hem, while some of the more extreme untucked ones go as high as

four yards. They are worn with the popular Basque waists. The fitted Basque illustrated, No. 8555, has either tucked or plain sleeves and two styles of collar and cuts in sizes 32 to 44 inches bust measure, requiring for size 36, 2 yards 36-inch material. The skirt, No. 8556, comes in size 22 to 32 inches waist measure, requiring in size 24, 6½ yards 36-inch material. Patterns 15 cents each.

8582—For the afternoon tea or the evening dance, one of the most up-to-date frocks, either for the matron or for the younger woman, is No. 8582, which may be made with a draped or dart-fitted Basque and with or without a draped sash. The tunic is suitable for lace or bordered chiffon and the underskirt has fan plaits at each side. It would be most striking if made of black velvet or satin and a white embroidered filet lace in bold design. The pattern cuts in sizes 34 to 42 inches bust measure, requiring in size 36, 3¾ yards 30-inch satin, with 2½ yards 7-inch lace for chemisette and sleeve cap, 2 yards 27-inch flouncing for tunic and 1¼ yards 36-inch lining. Pattern 15 cents.

EVEN THE NEW COATS HAVE TUNIC EFFECTS

8472—The present vogue for sharply contrasting materials is responsible for the popularity of shepherd check serge in combination with black satin, the materials in which dress 8472 is illustrated, though it would be equally attractive in a combination of two silks, a striped satin and a plain taffeta, for instance. The dress has a chemisette with standing collar and Byron tabs, full-length sleeves set into large armholes and a three-gored skirt with a three-piece box-plaited tunic, attached to a three-piece yoke. Pattern cuts in 6 sizes, 34 to 44 inches bust measure, size 36 requiring 4½ yards 36-inch serge, 2¾ yards 36-inch satin and 1⅝ yards 36-inch lining for underskirt. Price 15 cents.

8579—Tunic dresses are not only popular for street and afternoon but may be made up in ginghams or percales into the most up-to-date of house dresses. Such a dress is illustrated by 8579 whose pattern, cut in sizes 34 to 46 inches bust measure, includes a surplice waist with sleeves in either of two lengths and a three-piece tunic skirt with a four-gored tunic. Dress in size 36 will require 7⅞ yards 30-inch material, with ½ yard 27-inch contrasting goods, and 1¾ yards 36-inch lining. Price 15 cents.

8586-8587—The simple tailored dress of navy blue serge royal, trimmed in tailored fashion with military braid, is suitable either for house or street wear. Patterns No. 8586-8587 are illustrated in this combination, the former being a simple shirtwaist, with two styles of front-opening and full-length sleeves with flaring inset cuffs and standing collar, and the latter a two-gored semi-tunic skirt, with two-piece lining. Waist pattern cuts in sizes 32 to 46 inches bust measure and the skirt pattern in sizes 22 to 32 inches waist measure. The dress in medium size requires 5¼ yards 42-inch material with 1⅞ yards 30-inch lining. Patterns 15 cents each.

8579   8586-8587

8472

8570—Big loose coats of reversible blanketing are comfortable for motoring and traveling wear, and the materials for them come in a large variety of colors, including some soft and artistic shades of amethyst, green and gray. No. 8570 is such a coat and has heavy collars and cuffs and a big draped sash with pockets, or the coat may be made in shorter length, and with shawl collar, large patch pockets and, in this case, the shorter outline should be used and the belt omitted. Pattern cuts from 32 to 46 inches bust measure, requiring in size 36, 4¼ yards 54-inch reversible material. Price 15 cents.

8572-8535—The smartest of fall outlines are incorporated in Basque coat No. 8572 which may be made with box-plaited or circular tunic. With it is worn one of the popular box-plaited tunic skirts which may be made with or without circular ruffles at the foot, and with or without the draped sash. The coat pattern cuts in sizes 34 to 44 inches bust measure, requiring in size 36, 4⅜ yards 42-inch material, and the skirt pattern comes in sizes 22 to 32 inches waist measure, requiring 4 yards 36-inch satin and ⅞ yard 36-inch contrasting material and 2 yards 36-inch lining. Patterns 15 cents each.

8570

8572-8535

8472   8579   8586-8587   8572-8535   8570

YOUR HAIR—DOES IT NEED ATTENTION?

By MADGE P. WITHNELL

towel. However, if this be inconvenient, apply the oil to the scalp about half an hour before washing the hair.

Until the scalp is in good condition again, once every ten days is not too often in which to wash the head, providing the vaseline is applied once a week, or the night before the shampoo. Frequent washing is not, as many think, harmful, provided the hair is well-nourished and cared for between shampoos. This washing really depends upon the individual; in some cases the hair becomes soiled more quickly than in others, and so requires washing more often. For a healthy head of hair once every three or four weeks is enough.

When shampooing, use soft water if possible (rainwater is best); and for dark hair tar soap, while for

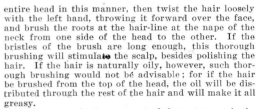

AFTER an unusually joyous and care-free summer in which no thought was given to such troublesome things as hats, and parasols were carried upon only very formal occasions, the hair naturally needs careful attention. We have perhaps also neglected to wash our heads thoroughly and free them from salt and dust when we returned from a swim or a ride. As a result of those few weeks of thoughtlessness the hair looks dead and lifeless. To bring it back to a healthy, glossy condition, nourishment is required, first of all. The best remedy is generally a simple one, so pure vaseline or olive oil will be first upon the list of beautifiers.

Just before going to bed, the hair must be combed out carefully to free it from tangles before this nourishment can be applied. When this has been done, place a good half teaspoonful of pure white vaseline upon a saucer. Dip the middle finger into the vaseline and rub this finger down the center parting. Then make a small parting as near to the first as possible and rub a little vaseline into this parting also. Repeat this operation around the head until the whole scalp has been benefited. If applied in this manner, the hair itself will not be greasy, but all the scalp will have been nourished. If possible allow this grease to remain on the scalp over night, and wash the head the next morning. During the night the pillow may be protected by a

light hair pure castile soap. The best way of making a shampoo is to scrape the bar of soap with a knife, letting the shavings fall into a small pitcher. Then pour boiling water over the soap, allowing it to dissolve. After it has cooled a little, use it just as you would a liquid shampoo. You will get more satisfactory results by this method than by rubbing the bar of soap on the hair; for frequently small pieces of soap stick to the strands and are difficult to remove without bringing some of the hair out with them.

Apply the shampoo to the scalp by pouring a little out on the hair and rubbing it in well with the fingers. Make a good lather by rubbing the fingertips gently but thoroughly back and forth on the scalp; do not, however, use the whole hand and rub the hair around, for this will not get the dirt out, but will only serve to tangle the hair into hopeless knots, and make it more difficult to take away the oil. After this has been rubbed thoroughly on the hair and scalp, hold the head over a basin or bath-tub, whichever you are using, and rinse off the soap by pouring warm water on the head. Then use more of the shampoo, repeating the process three or four times. Use plenty of clear, warm water when rinsing, finally using rather cool water, but not cold. The cooler water brings the blood to the scalp, invigorates it and prevents cold.

Dry your hair in a warm room with plenty of warm towels. The process of drying can be made considerably easier if you will waft the hair back and forth with a palm-leaf fan. Then comb the tangles out gently in the manner I have described; after which the hair is fanned again until dry. Another combing then ensues, before the hair is ready to do up.

Unless your hair is very oily, a good brushing once or twice a week will make it bright and glossy. If done in the following manner it will be beneficial to both your hair and scalp: After the hair is combed, part it in the center, dividing it again into small strands, and brush from the top of the head to the ends with long, straight strokes. Brush each strand separately, holding one side back while brushing the other. Go over the

entire head in this manner, then twist the hair loosely with the left hand, throwing it forward over the face, and brush the roots at the hair-line at the nape of the neck from one side of the head to the other. If the bristles of the brush are long enough, this thorough brushing will stimulate the scalp, besides polishing the hair. If the hair is naturally oily, however, such thorough brushing would not be advisable; for if the hair be brushed from the top of the head, the oil will be distributed through the rest of the hair and will make it all greasy.

Another very important part of the treatment is the massaging. Whether the scalp be dry or whether it be oily, this massage will be beneficial. In the former case, it stimulates the pores of the scalp so that the hair is nourished naturally, and in the latter case it checks the overabundance of oil and regulates its flow, by strengthening the pores.

When the hair has been combed out thoroughly, place the hands opposite each other upon the crown of the head, with the fingers spread apart and the tips placed firmly upon the scalp. Then push the hands together, still keeping the fingers in this position, thus moving the scalp but not rubbing nor injuring the hair. Do this all over the head—near the ears and from the back of the head to the forehead. This friction stimulates the growth of the hair by invigorating the scalp. If done for about ten minutes before retiring, it will be even more beneficial. If these different parts of the treatment are applied to your hair, in a comparatively short time you will see a marked improvement in your then glossy and beautiful locks.

CAPES, BASQUES AND TUNICS, FASHION'S FAVORITES

8355—One of the season's most popular silk dresses is illustrated by No. 8355, cut with kimono waist and draped vest and a two-piece skirt with gathered ruffles. Pattern cuts in sizes 34 to 42 inches bust measure, requiring in size 36, 6⅜ yards 30-inch material with 1½ yards 27-inch net and 1⅝ yards 36-inch lining. Price 15 cents.

8444—Pattern No. 8444 can be made up with a simple darted basque as illustrated or with a draped one as shown on the pattern envelope. The skirt is a straight gathered model with deep hem. Pattern cuts in sizes 34 to 42 inches bust measure and re-

quires in size 36, 4½ yards 36-inch material. Pattern 15 cents.

8531-8528—Smart circular capes of net are applied to any of the new foulard or taffeta dresses as in the illustration, where a cape waist in surplice style with full-length sleeves is combined with a three-piece gathered skirt with four flounces and a gathered yoke, any of which may be omitted. The waist pattern cuts in sizes 32 to 44 inches bust measure, the skirt in sizes 22 to 32 inches waist measure. Dress in medium size will require 9⅜ yards 30-inch material with ¾-yard 36-inch net for cape. Patterns 15 cents each.

8355

8444

8531
8528

8386
8430

8547
8549

8438
8496

8386-8430—A popular kimono blouse with full-length sleeves and deep corselet girdle and which may be made with peplums in pannier style, if desired, is shown in combination with a smart tunic skirt cut in three gores with a two-piece tunic and to be made without a yoke in girdle effect, as preferred. Waist pattern No. 8386 cuts in sizes 34 to 42 inches bust measure, and the skirt pattern, No. 8430, sizes 22 to 30 inches waist measure. Dress in medium size will require 3¾ yards 36-inch satin, 2¾ yards 42-inch serge and 2 yards 36-inch lining. Patterns 15 cents each.

8547-8549—An effective way for making up striped material is illustrated by patterns No. 8547-8549, the former, a loose-fitting coat with one of the new coachman's capes, and the latter a four-piece skirt with a circular tunic at the back. These garments are not only becoming to many figures but are so simple to make that they should have a wide appeal to the home dressmaker. The coat pattern cuts in sizes 32 to 42 inches bust measure, and the skirt in sizes 22 to 32 inches waist measure. For the suit in me-

dium size you will require 7¼ yards 42-inch material with ⅜ yard 36-inch satin. Patterns 15 cents each.

8438-8496—One of the novel, much-fitted coats, is shown in combination with an attractive Russian tunic skirt in cutaway outlines in Nos. 8438-8496. These are developed in a smart combination of Vendome blue serge royal with violet and blue striped serge and violet velvet for its collar and buttons. The coat pattern cuts in sizes 34 to 44 inches bust measure and the skirt in sizes 22 to 32 inches waist measure. For the suit in medium size you will require 4¾ yards 42-inch material with 1¼ yards 36-inch contrasting goods and ¼ yard 18-inch velvet for collar and 2 yards 36-inch lining. Patterns 15 cents each.

8355   8444   8531   8386   8547   8438
        8528   8430   8549   8496

SMART GODETS, FLOUNCES AND PLAITED SKIRTS

8533-8532—Short flaring capes decorate our newest coats, and Godet inserts our latest skirts, both of these features being shown in designs numbered 8533-8532. The pattern for the coat cuts in sizes 32 to 44 inches bust measure, requiring in size 36, 2½ yards 42-inch material with ¼ yard 42-inch contrasting material for the collar and cuffs, while the skirt pattern cuts in sizes 22 to 34 inches waist measure, requiring in size 24, 2⅝ yards 42-inch material with ¾ yard 42-inch contrasting goods for the Godet inserts. Patterns 15 cents each.

8525-8524—The plain conservative tailored coat is enjoying a revived popularity and combines well with the newest plaited skirts. The two patterns illustrated, which show these features, are numbered respectively 8525-8524. The coat, a semi-fitted model, with shawl or notched collar, and to be made with or without the belt, cuts in sizes 32 to 44 inches bust measure and requires, in size 36, 2⅝ yards 42-inch material with ¼ yard 18-inch contrasting goods for collar, and the skirt pattern cuts in sizes 22 to 32 inches waist measure, requiring in size 24, 3⅝ yards 42-inch material. Patterns 15 cents each.

8588-8581—Sleeveless overblouses are worn with many of the tunic skirts, as illustrated by numbers 8588-8581. In this case the overblouse is worn with a gathered guimpe opening in back, while the deep girdle repeats the material of the skirt's two-gored foundation. Waist pattern cuts in sizes 32 to 42 inches bust measure, and the skirt pattern in sizes 22 to 34 inches waist measure. The dress in medium size will require 3⅝ yards 36-inch material with 2⅜ yards 36-inch satin, 2 yards 42-inch net and 1¼ yards 27-inch lining. Patterns 15 cents each.

8527-8526—One of the popular vest waists is illustrated above in combination with the new full, double-flounced skirt. The waist pattern includes a removable chemisette and the skirt flounces may be made in straight or scalloped outlines at the lower edge. The waist pattern cuts for ladies and misses from 34 to 46 inches bust measure, requiring in size 36, 2⅛ yards 36-inch material with ⅞ yard 27-inch or ¾ yard 30-inch contrasting material. The skirt pattern cuts in sizes 22 to 30 inches waist measure, requiring in size 24, 6¼ yards 30-inch material. Patterns 15 cents each.

8480—One of the simplest of the new Russian tunic dresses is illustrated in No. 8480. The waist has inset vest and sleeves. The skirt has three-gored foundation and tunic. Pattern cuts from 34 to 42 inches bust measure, requiring in size 36, 3 yards 42-inch material with 1⅜ yards 36-inch contrasting material, ¼ yard 9-inch lace and 1½ yards 36-inch lining. Price 15 cents.

8533-8532   8525-8524

8588-8581

8527-8526

8480

8533
8532   8525
8524   8588
8581   8527
8526   8480

8529

8387

8588-8589

8574-8575

8536

THE NEW SKIRTS ARE SHOWING PLAITS

8529—An attractive Basque with a straight plaited tunic is illustrated by design No. 8529, developed in white serge, with collar, cuffs and underskirt-facing of Roman striped taffeta, a combination that is extremely popular at present. If desired the blouse and tunic could be made up and lined like a coat to wear with a skirt of contrasting material and a blouse of net and crêpe. In the illustration the skirt and overdress are made in one. Pattern cuts in five sizes, 32 to 40 inches bust measure, size 36 requiring 5⅛ yards 42-inch material with 2¼ yards 20-inch contrasting material and 1½ yards 27-inch lining. Price 15 cents.

8387—Plaid taffeta and black satin form the smart tunic dress illustrated above, with its kimono blouse, deep round collar and three-quarter length sleeves. Its center-front opening makes it especially practical as well as giving an opportunity for the use of decorative buttons. The pattern is cut in 5 sizes, from 34 to 42 inches bust measure, size 36 requiring 3 yards 36-inch plaid material, with 2¼ yards 36-inch satin and 1⅜ yards 27-inch lining. Pattern 15 cents.

8588-8589—Of the many fashionable overblouses one of the most attractive is the one illustrated in combination with a straight plaited skirt under Nos. 8588-8589. Made of soft poplin and worn over a filet net guimpe, it would be charming. The waist pattern cuts in sizes 32 to 42 inches bust measure and the skirt in sizes 22 to 32 inches waist measure, dress in medium size requiring 6 yards 36-inch material, with ¼ yard 36-inch satin and 2¼ yards 36-inch net. Patterns 15 cents each.

8574-8575—The simplest type of semi-fitted basque is illustrated in combination with one of the new accordion plaited tunic skirts. The arrangement of the sash is noteworthy, being fastened to the lower part of the basque, confining the fullness of the plaited tunic. Basque pattern cuts in sizes 32 to 46 inches bust measure, and the skirt in sizes 22 to 32 inches waist measure, the dress requiring in medium size 3⅛ yards 36-inch, with 4¼ yards 36-inch contrasting goods and 1¾ yards 36-inch lining. Patterns 15 cents each.

8536—Broadcloth of a soft dove grey is combined with satin of a deeper tone in making this attractive dress No. 8536. The waist is plain with long set-in sleeves gathered into deep band cuffs, and it has a duchess closing which is laced up with amethyst velvet ribbon and two collars, one of satin and the other of organdie. The tunic has a group of backward turning pleats at the side and it is mounted on a three-piece foundation skirt which may be faced part way up, if desired. Cut in 7 sizes, 32 to 44 inches bust measure, size 36 requiring 4¾ yards 42-inch material, with 1⅝ yards 36-inch satin and 1¾ yards 36-inch lining. Price 15 cents.

8529   8287   8588-8589   8574-8575   8536

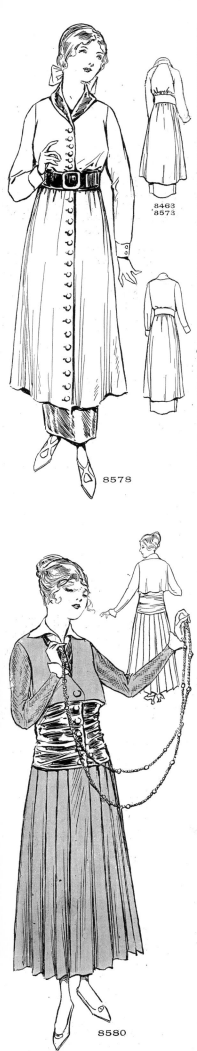

8463
8573

8578

8580

8463-8573

8584

8584

8465

8571

8578—For school or college wear No. 8578 would develop well in serge or taffeta, or in any of the light-weight fall woolens, with underskirt, collar and belt of satin or Roman striped silk. The blouse has a shawl collar and full-length sleeves, while the skirt is in two gores with a three-piece tunic. The pattern cuts in sizes 14, 16, 17 and 18 years, requiring in size 16, 3⅜ yards 42-inch material, with ⅞ yard 36-inch contrasting goods and 1⅝ yards 36-inch lining. Pattern 15 cents.

8580—Sleeveless boleros are being worn over many of the new Basque dresses and in many instances the plaited tunics have developed into real skirts as here illustrated. This can be made with a gathered girdle section or fitted Basque, and, of course, the bolero can be omitted when desired. The pattern cuts in sizes 16, 17 and 18 years, size 17 requiring 6⅛ yards 42-inch serge, with ⅞ yard 30-inch satin and ⅜ yard lawn. Pattern 15 cents.

8463-8573—Raglan waists are charming for girls, particularly in combination with tunic skirts such as the three-piece model with a gathered three-piece tunic illustrated. The waist pattern is cut in sizes 34 to 42 inches bust measure, requiring in size 36, 3 yards 30-inch material. The skirt pattern cuts in sizes 16, 17 and 18 years, requiring in size 18, 3¼ yards 42-inch material, with ⅝ yard 36-inch contrasting goods and 1⅞ yards 36-inch lining. Patterns 15 cents each.

8584—All sorts of flounced effects are being used for party dresses for young girls and nothing could be more youthful than a dress of this character in point d'esprit. The pattern for the dress illustrated has a surplice waist opening at the back, joined by a deep corselet girdle to a skirt with six graduated ruffles. Pattern cuts in sizes 16, 17 and 18 years, size 18 requiring 5⅝ yards 42-inch net, with 2½ yards 36-inch material for skirt, and ⅜ yard 36-inch silk for girdle. Pattern 15 cents.

8465—A clever little frock on the Salamander order is shown in No. 8465. Here the back of the blouse extends over the front in yoke effect and full-length sleeves are sewed into a drop-shouldered armscye. The three-piece skirt is almost hidden by the flaring tunic. The pattern cuts in sizes 14, 16, 17 and 18 years, size 16 requiring 3 yards 42-inch material, with 1⅛ yards 27-inch contrasting material and 1 yard 27-inch lining. Pattern 15 cents.

8571—One of the most popular of the Basque-tunic dresses is illustrated above in combination of black satin and plaid taffeta, which is popular this season. The pattern which has side-front closing, full-length sleeves, a three-piece foundation skirt, and a draped collar cuts in sizes 14, 16, 17 and 18 years, requiring in size 16, 4⅛ yards 42-inch material, with 1⅛ yards 36-inch contrasting goods for skirt facing and girdle and 1 yard 36-inch lining. Price 15 cents.

MISSES' DRESSES, COATS, CAPES AND SKIRT

*8424—Ladies' and Misses' One-piece Circular Raglan Coat. Collar may be worn three different ways. Coat perforated for shorter length. Sizes 32, 36, 40, 44. Size 36 requires 3⅞ yards 54-inch material. 15 cents.

*8438—Ladies' and Misses' Single-breasted Coat, in hip length, with full-length sleeves. Sizes 34, 36, 38, 40, 42, 44. Size 36 requires 2⅞ yards 36-inch or 2⅜ yards 42-inch material. 15 cents.

*8456—Ladies' and Misses' Cape, with vest and pointed collar. With or without circular frills on collar and cape. Sizes 32, 36, 40, 44. Size 36 requires 3 yards 42-inch material. 15 cents.

1½ yards wide   14 to 18

8465—Misses' Long-waisted Dress. Waist with back extending over to front in yoke effect, full-length or short sleeve. Skirt in three gores with three-piece tunic. Sizes 14, 16, 17, 18. Size 17 requires 3⅝ yards 36-inch material. 15 cents.

1⅝ yards wide
14 to 18

8462—Misses' Long-waisted Dress. To be made with or without suspender straps or inset box-plaits in skirt. Skirt in four gores slightly gathered at the waistline. Sizes 14, 16, 17, 18. Size 17 requires 5¼ yards 36-inch material. 15 cents.

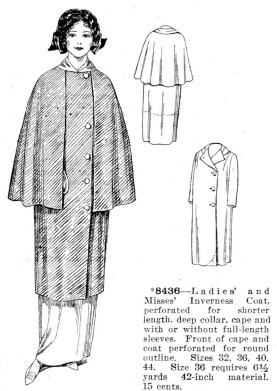

*8436—Ladies' and Misses' Inverness Coat, perforated for shorter length. deep collar, cape and with or without full-length sleeves. Front of cape and coat perforated for round outline. Sizes 32, 36, 40, 44. Size 36 requires 6½ yards 42-inch material. 15 cents.

8450—Ladies' and Misses' Coat with raglan sleeves. Round, flaring or deep collar in hood effect. Fullness in front held in by a belt. Sizes 34 to 42. Size 36 requires 3 yards 36-inch material. 15 cents.

*8445—Ladies' and Misses' Cape, in two lengths. 45-inch and 32 inches at center-back with hood and two styles of vest. Sizes 32, 36, 40, 44. Size 36 requires 4¼ yards 42-inch material. 15 cents.

1½ yards wide   16 to 18

8464—Misses' Skirt, in two gores with raised waistline. With or without two styles of long tunics and deep belt. Sizes 16, 17, 18. Size 17 requires 3¼ yards 36-inch material. 15 cents.

MISSES' TUNIC BASQUE AND RUFFLE DRESSES

1⅝ yards wide

7848—Misses' Dress, Waist in over-blouse effect, fastening on the shoulder, with large armhole, three-piece skirt and tunic with plaited panel front and back. Sizes 16, 17, 18. Size 16 requires 3½ yards 36-inch material. 15 cents.

8571
1⅝ yards wide

8584
1⅜ yards wide

8593—1½ yards wide

1⅝ yards wide—16 to 18

7843—Misses' Dress, with deep yoke in front that may be cut from tucked material, three-piece skirt with yoke, tuck and deep hem at foot. Sizes 16, 17, 18. Size 16 requires 4¼ yards 36-inch material. 15 cents.

8571—Misses' Basque Dress with full-length or shorter sleeves, and three-piece skirt with straight plaited tunic. Sizes 14, 16, 17, 18. Size 17 requires 6 yards 36-inch material. 15 cents.

8584—Misses' Flounced Dress. Surplice waist with set-in sleeves and gathered bertha. Skirt in three gores with straight gathered ruffles. Sizes 16, 17, 18. Size 17 requires 6⅜ yards 36-inch material. 15 cents.

8593—Misses' Basque Dress, with two collars. Three-piece foundation skirt with three-piece tunic. Sizes 16, 17, 18. Size 17 requires 4⅞ yards 36-inch material. 15 cents.

1½ yards wide
8578—Misses' Dress. Blouse opening in front with a shawl collar. Three-piece skirt with three-piece tunic. Sizes 14, 16, 17, 18. Size 17 requires 5⅛ yards 36-inch or 4⅝ yards 42-inch material. 15 cents.

1½ yards wide
8573—Misses' Tunic Skirt in three gores with a three-piece gathered tunic, to be worn with or without the belt, frill or trimming-bands. Sizes 16, 17, 18. Size 17 requires 3¼ yards 36-inch or 2¾ yards 42-inch material. 15 cents.

1½ yards wide
8580—Misses' Dress consisting of a basque waist with full-length sleeves. Straight plaited skirt and with or without the sleeveless bolero and crushed girdle. Sizes 16, 17, 18. Size 17 requires 7⅛ yards 36-inch material. 15 cents.

MISSES' LONG AND SHORT LENGTH COATS

*8572 — Ladies' and Misses' Basque Coat with Directoire collar, full-length sleeves with flaring cuffs and to be made either with or without a box-plaited or circular peplum. Sizes 34 to 44. Size 36 requires 5¼ yards 36-inch, or 4⅜ yards 42-inch material. 15 cents.

8539 — Ladies' and Misses' Directoire Coat with high turn-down collar, broad revers, deep peplum perforated for wide opening in front. Sizes 34, 36, 38, 40, 42. Size 36 requires 3⅜ yards 36-inch, 2⅞ yards 42-inch or 2⅜ yards 54-inch material. 15 cents.

8542 — Ladies' and Misses' Cape Coat, back in two lengths cut in one piece with the sleeve; semi-fitted vest with turn-over collar. Sizes 34, 36, 38, 40, 42. Size 36 requires 3 yards 36-inch, 2½ yards 42-inch or 2⅛ yards 54-inch material. 15 cents.

*8570—Ladies' and Misses' Long Coat in either of two lengths and with shawl or standing collar, two-piece sleeve with turned-back cuff and with or without crush belt. Sizes 32 to 46. Size 36 requires 5⅝ yards 42-inch or 4⅛ yards 54-inch material. 15 cents.

*8533 — Ladies' and Misses' Semi-fitted Coat. To be made with or without either of two capes and two-piece sleeves with turn-back cuffs. Sizes 32 to 44. Size 36 requires 3¾ yards 36-inch, 3¼ yards 42-inch or 2½ yards 54-inch material. 15 cents.

8547 — Ladies' and Misses' Coat with coachman cape, two-piece sleeve with turn-back cuff. Length of coat 34 inches. Sizes 32, 34, 36, 38, 40, 42. Size 36 requires 3⅞ yards 36-inch, 3½ yards 42-inch or 2¾ yards 54-inch material. 15 cents.

8559—Ladies' and Misses' Sleeveless Coatee worn over a belted blouse with full-length bell sleeve that may be plaited at the wrist, turned-down collar and pointed peplum. Sizes 32 to 42. Size 36 requires 2 yards 36-inch or 1¾ yards 42-inch material. 15 cents.

*8525 — Ladies' and Misses' Single-breasted Cutaway Coat with shawl or notched collar and with or without belt. Sizes 32, 34, 36, 38, 40, 42, 44. Size 36 requires 3⅛ yards 36-inch, 2¾ yards 42-inch or 2¼ yards 54-inch material. 15 cents.

MISSES' DRESSES, COATS, CAPES AND CAPE COATS

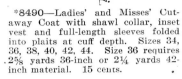

8502—Ladies' and Misses' Single-breasted Coat with rolling collar and full-length sleeves with turn-back cuffs. Sizes 34, 36, 38, 40, 42. Size 36 requires 3⅛ yards 36-inch, 2⅝ yards 42-inch or 2⅛ yards 54-inch material. 15 cents.

*8490—Ladies' and Misses' Cutaway Coat with shawl collar, inset vest and full-length sleeves folded into plaits at cuff depth. Sizes 34, 36, 38, 40, 42, 44. Size 36 requires 2⅝ yards 36-inch or 2¼ yards 42-inch material. 15 cents.

*8512—Ladies' and Misses' Long Cape, gathered into a small shaped yoke to which is attached a flaring collar. Cape to be worn with or without the fitted vest. Sizes 32, 36, 40, 44. Size 36 requires 3⅜ yards 42-inch material. 15 cents.

*8477—Ladies' and Misses' Circular Military Cape. May be made of reversible material, straight or shaped at lower edge and with a turn-down collar. Sizes 32, 36, 40, 44. Size 36 requires 5 yards 42-inch or 3¾ yards 54-inch material. 15 cents.

1⅝ yards wide

1⅞ yards wide

*8479—Ladies' and Misses' Three-quarter length Coat slightly eased to shallow yoke in front and with turned down collar, turn-back cuffs and a three-piece girdle. Sizes 34, 36, 38, 40, 42, 44. Size 36 requires 4 yards 42-inch material. 15 cents.

8468—Misses' Dress, waist-lining with V-neck, pointed collar and perforated for low neck. Skirt in three gores with tunic having three gathered tucks. Sizes 16, 17, 18. Size 17 requires 4¾ yards 36-inch material. 15 cents.

8474—Misses' Dress with raised waistline. Kimono waist with elbow sleeves and gathered tucker. Skirt in three gores and having four gathered ruffles. Sizes 16, 17, 18. Size 17 requires 3½ yards 36-inch material. 15 cents.

*8475—Ladies' and Misses' Cape Coat consisting of a round box coat with a short sailor collar and two-piece sleeves with turn-back cuffs and a deep circular cape. Sizes 32, 36, 40, 44. Size 36 requires 5¼ yards 42-inch material. 15 cents.

VARIOUS STYLE DRESSES FOR YOUNG GIRLS

7924—Misses' Peasant Dress. Blouse with short sleeve, draped overblouse; three-piece skirt and two-piece tunic. Sizes 16, 17, 18. Size 16 requires of one material 3½ yards 36 inches wide. 15 cents.

16 to 18
1⅝ yards wide

*8383—Ladies' and Misses' Apron Dress, elbow sleeves. Front of waist cut in one with hip yoke that forms pocket. Sizes 32, 36, 40, 44, 48. Size 36 requires 5½ yards 36-inch material. 15 cents.

32 to 48
1¾ yards wide

7841—Misses' Peasant Dress, Russian blouse and skirt, blouse closing at the sideback. Sizes 14, 16, 17, 18. Width at lower edge in size 16, 1⅜ yards. Size 16 requires 5 yards 36-inch material. 15 cents.

14 to 18
1⅜ yards wide

8380—Misses' Dress. Waist with draped collar, chemisette. Skirt in four gores. Sizes 14, 16, 17, 18. Size 16 requires 4⅛ yards 36-inch material. 15 cents.

14 to 18
1½ yards wide

8388—Misses' Dress. Waist with raglan sleeve, chemisette, round collar extending into revers; skirt in three gores. Sizes 14, 16, 17, 18. Size 16 requires 4⅛ yards 36-inch material. 15 cents.

14 to 18
1⅝ yards wide

8374—Misses' Dress. Blouse with two dart tucks in front; skirt in three gores with circular flounce. Sizes 16, 17, 18. Size 16 requires 5½ yards 36-inch material. 15 cents.

16 to 18
1⅜ yards wide

FOR SCHOOL AND PARTY WEAR

8576—A practical model is illustrated under number 8576. It is a one-piece dress made to slip on over the head and when worn with a patent leather belt and a white linen collar it would be attractive for school wear. The pattern comes in 5 sizes from 2 to 10 years, and size 10 will require 3 yards 30-inch material. Price 15 cents.

8585—Box plaits are fashionable again and in this dress the full box-plaited skirt is buttoned onto a long-waisted box-plaited waist. The pattern comes in sizes 4 to 10 years and requires for size 12, 1¾ yards 27-inch material for skirt, belt, collar and cuffs and 2⅛ yards 27-inch material for the waist. Price 15 cents.

8564—Girls' surplice overblouse dress opening in front. Two-piece circular skirt with two-piece circular tunic. Pattern comes in sizes 6 to 12 years requiring for size 10, 2¾ yards 30-inch material for overblouse and skirt and 1¾ yards 30-inch material for guimpe. Price 15 cents.

14606—Three Bulgarian Borders ½, ⅝, and ¾ inch wide respectively. 3 yards and 4 corners of each in the pattern. Price 10 cents.

8534—Here is a practical little garment for wear out of doors. It is cut in peasant style and its double-breasted front gives plenty of warmth. The pattern is cut in sizes 1 to 6 years and size 6 will require 3¼ yards 27-inch with ¾ yard 27-inch or wider material for collar, trimming bands and the belt. Price 15 cents.

8142—The Oliver Twist suit which is illustrated under the number of 8142, consists of a box-plaited shirtwaist with full-length sleeves, turn-back cuffs and round collar and straight trousers which are made to button on to the waistband, making it very practical for laundry purposes. Pattern cuts from 4 to 10 years and for size 4 you will require 2⅛ yards 36-inch goods if made all of one material. Price 15 cents.

8583—Even the little tots are wearing the Basque coat and the plaited skirt as is shown in the illustration. This coat is single-breasted and has two styles of collar and cuff. This would be attractive developed in serge, broadcloth or gabardine. The pattern comes in 4 sizes from 4 to 10 years and requires for size 8, 2⅞ yards 36-inch material. Price 15 cents.

8576

8446

8585

8564
Emb. 14606

8583

8534

8142

8544

8446—Some clever designer has adapted the boys' Oliver Twist suit for his big sister, and an attractive version of this style is shown in the illustration. The skirt, collar and cuffs are of plaid gingham and the waist may be of batiste, piqué or linen. This would also be attractive made of plaid and plain serge in the darker colorings for fall and winter wear. The pattern comes in 6 sizes from 2 to 12 years and will require for size 12, 2½ yards 30-inch material with 1½ yards 30-inch plain material for waist and sleeves. Price 15 cents.

8544—A very dainty and charming little party dress developed in white net and worn over a slip of silk is illustrated in No. 8544. The edges of the ruffles may be finished with a picot edge or with a tiny Val. lace insertion and the girdle and bows of ribbon on the shoulder should be of blue satin to match the ribbon girdle. A wreath of pink roses is used to slip the girdle through. The pattern comes in 4 sizes from 8 to 14 years and will require for size 8, 3¾ yards 42-inch net with 2¼ yards 5-inch satin ribbon. Price 15 cents.

CHILDREN'S DRESSES FOR ANY OCCASION

$\frac{1}{2}$ to 5

2 to 8

1 to 6

$\frac{1}{2}$ to 6

8437—Child's Dress to be made of any soft material, to be tucked or gathered with front panel extending into yoke, high or round neck and full-length sleeves perforated for elbow length. Sizes $\frac{1}{2}$, 1, 2, 3, 4, 5. Size 3 requires $2\frac{1}{8}$ yards 27-inch, 2 yards 30-inch or $1\frac{7}{8}$ yards 36-inch material with long sleeves. 10 cents.

8553—Child's Empire Dress gathered to a square yoke back and front, full-length sleeves perforated for elbow length, full gathered skirt with two tucks and a deep hem. To be worn with or without sash. Sizes 2, 4, 6, 8. Size 4 requires $2\frac{3}{8}$ yards 30-inch, $2\frac{1}{4}$ yards 36-inch material. 15 cents.

8551—Child's Bishop Dress to be gathered to a round yoke with or without flat collar and cuffs, or rows of shirring in yoke and cuff effect. Two tucks in skirt and deep hem. Sizes 1, 2, 3, 4, 5, 6. Size 4 requires $3\frac{3}{8}$ yards 27-inch, $3\frac{1}{4}$ yards 30-inch or $2\frac{7}{8}$ yards 36-inch material. 15 cents.

8452—Child's Dress, to be made of any soft material, and trimmed with insertion and edging, with fronts and back gathered at neck, standing collar or round neck, full-length sleeve perforated for elbow length. Sizes $\frac{1}{2}$, 1, 2, 3, 4, 5, 6. Size 3 requires 2 yards 27-inch or 30-inch, or $1\frac{7}{8}$ yards 36-inch material. 10 cents.

2 to 12

6 to 14

4 to 14

8 to 14

2 to 14

8446—Girls' Dress, consisting of a waist with round collar, and two-piece skirt with inverted plait at each side, patch pockets. Skirt and waist to be attached at slightly high waistline with buttons and buttonholes. Sizes 2, 4, 6, 8, 10, 12. Size 8 requires $1\frac{3}{4}$ yards 36-inch material. 15 cents.

8546—Girls' Suspender Dress with kimono guimpe gathered at the neck in front, full-length sleeve perforated for elbow length, suspender overblouse and three-piece plaited skirt. Sizes 6, 8, 10, 12, 14. Size 10 requires $3\frac{1}{4}$ yards 27-inch, $3\frac{1}{8}$ yards 30-inch or $2\frac{5}{8}$ yards 36-inch material. 15 cents.

8548—Girls' Long-waisted Tunic Dress to slip on over the head, with sailor collar and removable chemisette, full-length sleeve with turn-back cuffs perforated for shorter length and two-piece skirt with two-piece circular tunic. Sizes 4 to 14. Size 10 requires $4\frac{1}{8}$ yards 30-inch material. 15 cents.

8544—Girls' Ruffled Dress with round neck and elbow sleeves and one-piece gathered skirt. To be made with or without the gathered ruffles which may be made of lace. Sizes 8, 10, 12, 14. Size 10 requires $5\frac{3}{4}$ yards 27-inch, $4\frac{5}{8}$ yards 36-inch or $4\frac{1}{8}$ yards 42-inch material. 15 cents.

8449—Girls' Kimono Apron Dress, closing at the back, with elbow sleeves, flat collar and front panel forming pockets. Sizes 2, 4, 6, 8, 10, 12, 14. Size 8 requires $3\frac{1}{4}$ yards 27-inch, $2\frac{3}{4}$ yards 30-inch material with $\frac{3}{8}$ yard 30-inch or 36-inch contrasting material for collar and sleeve facing. 10 cents.

MISCELLANEOUS CHILDREN'S WEAR

1 to 14

8431—Child's One-piece Night-gown, to slip on over the head. Sizes 1, 2, 3, 4, 5, 6, 8, 10, 12 14. Size 8 requires 2½ yards 30-inch material. 10 cents.

1 to 14

8440—Girl's Sack Apron, with full-length or short sleeves. Sizes 1, 2, 3, 4, 5, 6, 8, 10, 12, 14. Size 6 requires 2⅛ yards 30-inch material. 10 cents.

1 to 14

8426—Child's Long or Short Peasant Kimono. Sizes 1, 2, 3, 4, 5, 6, 8, 10, 12, 14. Size 8 requires 3¾ yards 30-inch material. 10 cents.

2 to 14

8448—Girl's Kimono with yoke and sleeve in one. Sizes 2, 3, 4, 5, 6, 8, 10, 12, 14. Size 8 requires 3 yards 30-inch material. 10 cents.

4 to 14

8457—Girl's Single-breasted Raglan Coat that may be closed high or low at neck in front. Sizes 4, 6, 8, 10, 12, 14. Size 10 requires 2⅝ yards 42-inch material. 15 cents.

8371—Girl's Short Coat, with raglan sleeves, sailor collar. Sizes 4, 6, 8, 10, 12, 14. Size 8 requires 1¾ yards 36-inch material, with ⅜ yard 27-inch or wider contrasting material. 15 cents.

One Size

8455—Infants' Dress, in 36-inch length perforated for 28 inches. One size only, and requires in long length 2¼ yards 36-inch material. 10 cents.

4 to 14

8439—Boys' Double-breasted Raglan Overcoat, to be made with or without pockets or belt. Sizes 4, 6, 8, 10, 12, 14. Size 10 requires 2⅞ yards 42-inch material. 15 cents.

½ to 6

8442—Child's Rompers, long or short sleeves, round or low neck. Sizes ½, 1, 2, 3, 4, 5, 6. Size 3 requires 2⅝ yards 30-inch material. 10 cents.

4 to 14

8459—Girl's Coat. Sizes 4 to 14. Size 10 requires 2⅝ yards 42-inch material. 15 cents.

½ to 6

8434—Child's Coat, with round collar, circular cape and deep belt. Sizes ½ to 6. Size 4 requires 2⅝ yards 36-inch material. 10 cents.

½ to 6

8443—Child's Double-breasted Coat, with round collar, full-length sleeve, circular cape and belt. Sizes ½ to 6. Size 4 requires 2¾ yards 36-inch material. 10 cents.

SCHOOL AND HOME CLOTHES FOR ACTIVE YOUNGSTERS

6576—Boys' double-breasted norfolk suit; coat and knickerbockers. Pattern cuts in sizes 6 to 14 years, size 10 requiring 3¾ yards, 36-inch material, with ⅜ yard 36-inch contrasting material for collar and belt. Pattern 15 cents.

7180—Boys' knickerbockers, with leg bands and elastics and fly or facing. Pattern cuts in sizes 4 to 14 years, size 8 requiring 1½ yards 30-inch material. Pattern 10 cents.

7612—Girls' middy dress, blouse and skirt. Cuts in 5 sizes, 6, 8, 10, 12 and 14, size 10 requiring 4¾ yards 36-inch material with ¾ yard 27-inch lining for underwaist. Pattern 15 cents.

7750—Girls' one-piece dress in long-waisted style, with inset yoke, slightly low round neck. Sizes 4 to 12 years, size 8 requiring 2½ yards 30-inch material with 2 yards 36-inch contrasting goods. Pattern 15 cents.

7792—Boys' sailor suit, blouse and knickerbockers or plain trousers, blouse with sailor collar. Cuts in sizes 4 to 10 years, size 8 requiring 3 yards 36-inch material with 3½ yards braid. Pattern 15 cents.

7951   7612   7750   8028

7951—Girls' peasant dress with separate guimpe. Shaped yoke and sleeves cut in one. Cuts in sizes 4 to 10 years, size 8 requiring 3½ yards 30-inch material with 1¼ yards 36-inch material for guimpe. Pattern 15 cents.

8001—Boys' dress with raglan sleeve. Dress made full-length and perforated for shorter length to be worn with bloomers. Sizes ½ to 4 years, size 2 requiring 1⅞ yards 30-inch material. Pattern 15 cents.

8028—Girls' one-piece dress closing at center front, with adjustable trimming tabs. Cuts in sizes 4 to 12 years, size 8 requiring 2⅜ yards 30-inch material with ½ yard 27-inch contrasting material. Pattern 15 cents.

8032—Girls' coat, in long waist effect with diagonal closing, and collar forming a point on the shoulders. Cuts in 5 sizes from 2 to 10 years, medium size requiring 2⅜ yards 36-inch material. Pattern 15 cents.

8132—Girls' sports-coat in raglan effect with sleeves cut in one with back, turn down collar, broad belt and pockets. Cuts in sizes 6 to 14 years, size 10 requiring 2½ yards 36-inch material. Pattern 15 cents.

8194—Boys' Russian suit, blouse fastening under the front trimming piece. Full length sleeve perforated for shorter length. Cuts in sizes 2 to 6 years, size 4 requires 2½ yards 30-inch material. Pattern 10 cents.

8238—Girls' kimono coat with diagonal closing and with sleeve and front yoke cut in one with the back. Pattern cuts in sizes 8 to 14 years, size 12 requiring 4¼ yards 30-inch material. Pattern 15 cents.

8032   8238   8132

8032

8238   8132   7951   7612   7750   8028

8001   8194   6576   7792   7180

8001   8194   6576   7792   7180

SIMPLICITY IS THE KEYNOTE FOR CHILDREN

8548   8544   8142   8546

8541   8534   8538

8541   8534   8538   8446   8457

8541—A dress for the small boy is illustrated in No. 8541. A peasant blouse with panel front and back, square collar and full-length sleeves perforated for shorter length is worn with a pair of full knickerbockers. The pattern cuts in ½, 1, 2, 3 and 4 years, size 2 requiring 2⅞ yards 27-inch material. Price 15 cents.

8534—For small children the peasant coats are the simplest things to make. The one illustrated closes at the side-front and has a small round collar and full-length sleeves. The pattern is cut in sizes 1, 2, 3, 4, 5 and 6, size 4 requiring 3¼ yards of 30-inch material with ¾ yard 27-inch material. Price 15 cents.

8538—A simple dress for the tiny boy, is shown in this number. The blouse has a tuck at the armscye and closes under a box-plait, while the full-length sleeves are perforated for shorter length. The pattern is cut in 1, 2, 3, 4, 5 and 6 years, size 4 years requiring 3⅜ yards of 27-inch material. Price 15 cents.

8546—Suspender dresses are always practical and comfortable for the little tots, particularly when the guimpe is on the kimono order as in dress No. 8546, which has a three-piece plaited skirt and a deep belt. The pattern is cut from 6 to 14 years, and size 10 will require 3¼ yards 27-inch material with 1¼ yards 36-inch goods for the guimpe. Price 15 cents.

8446—Nothing could be simpler for little girls than the practical dress illustrated here, with its convenient pockets and its simple blouse in shirtwaist style. The pattern is cut in 6 sizes from 2 to 12 years and in size 8, if made from two materials will require 1⅞ yards 30-inch material for the collar, cuffs and skirt and 1¼ yards 30-inch material for waist. Price 15 cents.

8457—Raglan coats are popular for girls particularly when they may be closed high in the neck. They work out well in reversible coatings or in homespuns. The pattern is cut in 6 sizes, 4 to 14 years requiring for size 10, 2⅝ yards 42-inch material without up and down, and ½ yard 27-inch contrasting material. Price 15 cents.

8548   8544   8142   8546   8446   8457

8548—Long-waisted tunic dresses are popular for little girls. No. 8548 is an excellent one and is made to slip on over the head. The two-piece skirt has a two-piece tunic. The pattern is cut from 4 to 14 years, size 8 requiring 3 yards 36-inch material. Price 15 cents.

8544—Ruffles and flounces are popular for the little girl as well as her older sister as shown by this charming example. The pattern is cut from 8 to 14 years. Size 12 requiring 2⅝ yards of 36-inch material with 2¼ yards 36-inch contrasting goods for ruffles. Price 15 cents.

8142—Boys' Oliver Twist suit consisting of shirtwaist with applied box-plait and straight trousers buttoning at the sides and to the shirtwaist. The pattern cuts from 4 to 10 years. Size 6 requires 2½ yards 30-inch goods if made all of one material. Price 15 cents.

PRACTICAL SCHOOL CLOTHES FOR BOYS AND GIRLS

8446—This modification of a boy's Oliver Twist suit for a girl consists of a waist with V-neck, round collar, full-length sleeves and a two-piece skirt with inverted plait at each side and patch pockets. Pattern comes from 2 to 12 years, size 8 requiring 1¾ yards 36-inch material, with 1 yard 36-inch material for waist. Price 15 cents.

8142—Boy's Oliver Twist suit, consisting of a shirtwaist with applied box-plaits and straight trousers, opening at the sides and to be buttoned to the shirt-waist. It cuts in sizes 4, 6, 8 and 10 years, requiring for size 8, 2¾ yards 30-inch material, with ¼ yard contrasting material for collar and cuffs. Price 15 cents.

8185—Sailor suits are always excellent for school wear. This one has a short belted blouse, straight trousers and full-length sleeve perforated for shorter length. Pattern cuts in 4 sizes, from 2 to 8 years, size 4 requiring 2 yards 36-inch material, with ½ yard 36-inch contrasting material and 8 yards soutache braid for trimming. Price 15 cents.

8476

8446   8142   8185

8476—Serge, cheviot and covet cloth, as well as various weaves of coat mixtures are suitable for this boy's double-breasted overcoat, which has full-length sleeve, having turn-back cuffs, small round collar and patch pockets. Pattern cuts in 7 sizes, from 6 to 14 years, requiring for size 8 years, 2¼ yards 42-inch material. Price 15 cents.

8321—Serge, flannel, galatea cloth and linen are all suitable for this box-plaited dress which is made to slip on over the head and has full-length sleeves. It can be worn with or without the shield and belt. The pattern comes in 7 sizes, from 2 to 14 years, requiring for size 8, 3 yards 30-inch material, with ½ yard 36-inch contrasting. Price 15 cents.

7437-7180

7437-7180—The shirt pattern No. 7437 comes for men and boys in sizes 26 to 44 and will require for size 28, 3¾ yards 27-inch material. The boy's knickerbockers, No. 7180, are cut with leg bands, fly and facing. The pattern comes in 6 sizes, from 4 to 14 years, and will require in size 8, 1½ yards 30, 36 or 42-inch material. Price 15 cents each.

8481—Cape coats for children are very popular as shown by the drawing illustrating coat No. 8481. It has patch pockets, full-length sleeve and circular cape and round collar in hood effect. The pattern cuts in 7 sizes, from 2 to 14 years, requiring for size 10, 3⅝ yards 42-inch double-faced coating. Price 15 cents.

8321

8481

8319—Serge dresses worn with patent leather belts and white linen collar and cuffs are very popular for school wear. This dress closes at the back and the pattern contains a deep draped sash, full-length sleeve and detachable collar. The pattern cuts in 4 sizes, from 4 to 10 years and will require for size 8, 2⅛ yards 36-inch material. Price 15 cents.

8495—Long-waisted dresses are stylish for the little tots. This dress closes in front and has a round collar, full-length sleeve, perforated for elbow length, deep belt and straight plaited skirt. The pattern cuts in sizes 2 to 10 years and will require for size 6, 2⅞ yards 30-inch material, with ⅝ yard 30-inch contrasting material. Price 15 cents.

COATS AND SUITS FOR BOYS

8142—4 to 10

6275—2 to 6

6618—2 to 8

7366—2 to 6

7884 4 to 10

7130 2 to 6

8142—Boys' Oliver Twist Suit, consisting of shirt-waist and straight trousers buttoning at the sides, and to be buttoned to the shirt-waist. Sizes 4, 6, 8, 10. Size 8 requires 2¾ yards 30-inch or 2¼ yards 36-inch material. 15 cents.

6275—Boys' Double-breasted Overcoat, with two-piece sleeve. To be made with or without pockets. Sizes 2, 4, 6, 8, 10. Size 8 requires 2¼ yards 44-inch or 1¾ yards of 54-inch material. 15 cents.

7884—Double-breasted Overcoat, suitable for girls and boys, with round collar, and full-length two-piece sleeve, deep belt, inverted plait at center-back. Sizes 4, 6, 8, 10. Size 6 requires 2⅛ yards 42-inch material. 15 cents.

7901—Boys' Double-breasted Overcoat, with sailor collar, perforated for shawl collar, and full-length two-piece sleeve. To be made with or without belt at back. Sizes 2, 4, 6, 8, 10. Size 6 requires 2 yards 36-inch, 1⅞ yards 42-inch or 1½ yards 54-inch material. 15 cents.

8316—Boys' Sailor Suit, blouse and knicker-bockers. Blouse with full-length sleeve and shaped yoke back and front. Sizes 4, 6, 8, 10, 12. Size 8 requires 3⅝ yards 27-inch, 3⅛ yards 30-inch, or 2⅝ yards 36-inch material, and ⅝ yard 18-inch contrasting material for sailor collar, etc. 15 cents.

7366—Boys' Suit, blouse and trousers. Blouse closing at the shoulder and side-front, with a square neck, and full-length sleeve with band cuff that may be cut off for shorter length. Sizes 2, 4, 6. Size 4 requires 2½ yards 36-inch material. 15 cents.

6618—Boys' Russian Blouse Suit, with knick-erbockers or plain trousers. Blouse closing diagonally in front, with full-length sleeve plaited in cuff effect, and perforated for shorter length. Sizes 2, 4, 6, 8. Size 4 requires 2¾ yards 36-inch material, with 1 yard contrasting material. 15 cents.

7130—Boys' Single-breasted Overcoat, with round or military collar, two-piece sleeve. To be made with or without turn-back cuffs or pockets. Sizes 2, 4, 6. Size 4 requires 1¾ yards 42-inch material. 15 cents.

7799—Boys' Double-breasted Coat, notched collar and full-length two-piece sleeve. With or without turn-back cuff, or belt at back. Sizes 2, 4, 6, 8, 10. Size 6 requires 2¼ yards 36 or 2 yards 42-inch material. 15 cents.

8240—Boys' Double-breasted Reefer Coat, having a notched collar and a sailor collar. Full-length two-piece sleeve. Sizes 4, 6, 8, 10. Size 8 requires 2 yards 36-inch, 1⅞ yards 42-inch or 1⅜ yards 54-inch material. 15 cents.

7901—2 to 10

8316—4 to 12

7799   2 to 10

8240 4 to 10

PRACTICAL WEAR FOR MEN AND BOYS

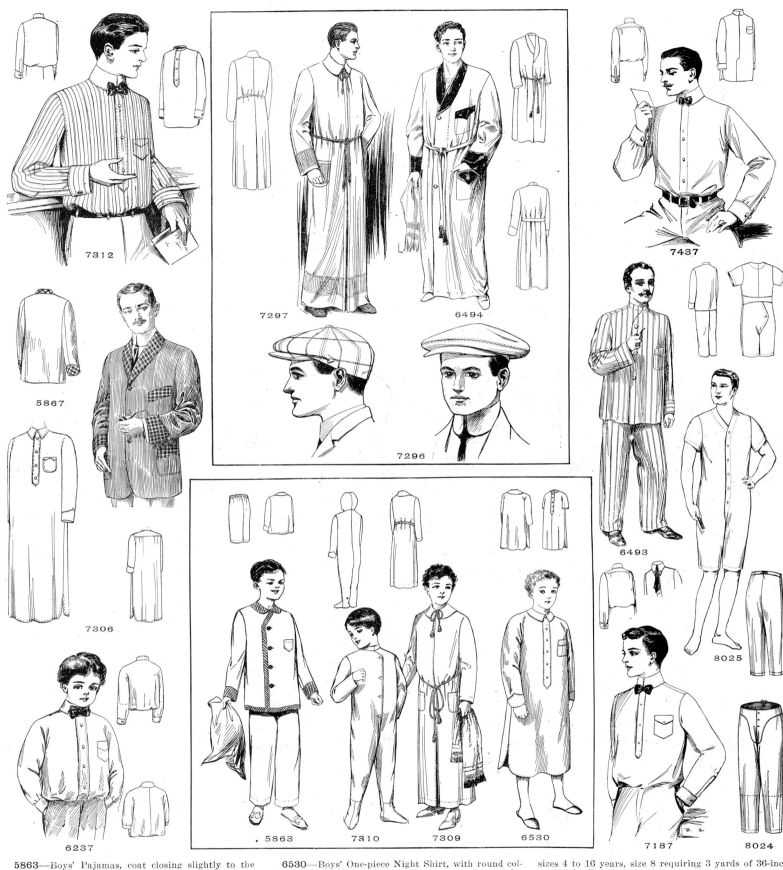

5863 — Boys' Pajamas, coat closing slightly to the side-front, with round collar and full-length sleeves, perforated for three-quarter length. Sizes 4 to 12 years, and size 8 requires 4 yards 30-inch material, with ½ yard 27-inch contrasting goods. Price 15 cents.

5867 — Men's Single-breasted House Coat. Sizes 34 to 46. Size 36 requires 3¼ yards 44-inch material. 15 cents.

6237 — Boys' Peasant Blouse, with box-pleat at center-front, full-length sleeve perforated for elbow length, round collar. Sizes 4 to 12 years, size 8 requiring 2 yards 30-inch material. Price 10 cents.

6493 — Men's and Boys' Pajamas, with high neck. Sizes 26 to 46. Size 30 requires 6 yards 30-inch or 5 yards 36-inch material. 15 cents.

6494 — Men's Bathrobe. Sizes 34, 38, 42, 46. Size 38 requires 6½ yards 36-inch material. 15 cents.

6530 — Boys' One-piece Night Shirt, with round collar or collarless, and full-length sleeve, perforated for shorter length. To be made with or without pocket, or cuff on full-length sleeve. Cuts in sizes 2 to 12 years, size 8 requiring 3¼ yards 30-inch material. Price 10 cents.

7187 — Men's and Boys' Négligée Shirt. Sizes 28 to 46. Size 36 requires 3½ yards 36-inch material. 15 cents.

7296 — Men's and Boys' Caps. Sizes 6¾, 7, 7¼. Any size requires ½ yard 36-inch material. 10 cents.

7297 — Men's Bathrobe. Sizes 34, 38, 42, 46. Size 38 requires 4½ yards 42-inch material. 15 cents.

7306 — Men's and Boys' Night Shirt. Sizes 26 to 50. Size 36 requires 3¾ yards 40-inch material. 15 cents.

7309 — Boys' Bathrobe, with round collar, full-length two-piece sleeve, and with or without pockets. Cuts in sizes 4 to 16 years, size 8 requiring 3 yards of 36-inch material. Price 15 cents.

7310 — Outdoor Sleeping Robe for Ladies and Misses, Men and Boys. Sizes for men and boys, 31, 33, 37, 41, 45. Size 33 requires 4¾ yards 36-inch material. 15 cents.

7312 — Men's and Boys' Négligée Shirt, shirt sleeve with French cuff. Sizes 26 to 44. Size 34 requires 3½ yards 30-inch or 3 yards 36-inch material. 15 cents.

7437 — Men's and Boys' Coat Shirt, with lap closing. Sizes 26 to 44. Size 34 requires 3¾ yards 30-inch or 3 yards 36-inch material. 15 cents.

8024 — Men's Drawers. 8 sizes, 30 to 44. Size 40 requires 3¼ yards 36-inch material. 15 cents.

8025 — Men's Union Suit. 8 sizes, 34 to 48. Size 40 requires 3¼ yards 36-inch material. 15 cents.

FOR EMBROIDERING WAISTS AND COLLARS

14668—This collar may be worn flat or standing. Three designs in pattern. 15 cents.

14681—Design for standing collar, vest and cuffs of lawn or batiste. 15 cents.

14664—A dainty rose and forget-me-not design for embroidering a waist. The pattern contains transfers for stamping front of waist, collar, cuffs and two extra sprays. This design, which is illustrated on waist 7715, should be developed in solid work, eyelets, outline and seed-stitch. Handkerchief linen, lawn, cotton crêpe or crêpe de Chine may be used for making this waist, which is cut in six sizes. 15 cents each.

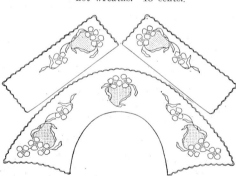

14664—Waist design of rose and forget-me-not wreaths. 15 cents.

14653—Conventional flower design for embroidering waist. This design, which includes sprays for the front of a waist, collar and cuffs, may be worked in one or more colors. It is effective developed in outline-stitch and solid work, on waists of chiffon, crêpe de Chine or handkerchief linen, or in appliqué on net. This design is illustrated on waist, 8109, which comes in 6 sizes. 15 cents.

14646—Futurist collar and cuff set, to be embroidered in purple, blue, vermilion, orange, green and black on ratine, linen or crêpe de Chine. 15 cents.

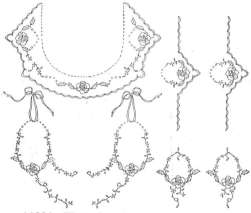

14615—Punched work design for collar and cuffs. The flowers may be developed in solid work or Italian relief stitch in white or a color. 15 cents.

14560—This design for a collar and cuff set should be stamped on fine lawn or handkerchief linen and developed in cut work or buttonhole-stitch in white. This set is suitable for wear with a suit or dress. 15 cents.

14643—These designs for collars and cuffs may be developed in one or more colors on colored linen, ratine, crêpe de Chine or handkerchief linen. 15 cents.

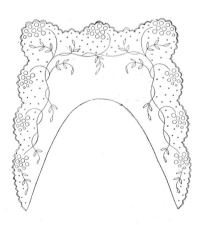

14653—Futurist design for embroidering waist of linen, silk or wool in one or more colors. 15 cents.

14241—Sailor collar. Suitable for wear with suit or dress. This design should be stamped on fine handkerchief linen and embroidered in solid work and eyelets with white mercerized cotton. 15 cents.

TRIMMINGS FOR PARTY DRESSES

7837
Emb. 14533

8468
Emb. 14312

8584
Emb. 14563

8544
Emb. 14553

8355
Emb. 14105-14104

8582
Emb. 12700-14182

12700—Developed in braid, this makes an effective trimming for the basque dress, 8582. This border is 11 inches wide, pattern contains one yard for 10 cents. The border used on the sleeve, 14182, is of a similar design. It is five inches wide and pattern contains 2¼ yards. The dress comes in sizes 34 to 42 inches. 15 cents each.

14105—This braiding border, 2½ inches wide, is suitable for trimming dresses or suits. 3 yards are contained in the pattern for 10 cents. The motifs, in pattern 14104, may be used with this border, as shown on dress 8355, which comes in sizes 34 to 42 inches. 15 cents each.

14533—French knots, solid embroidery and lace insertion was used in developing this design which makes an attractive trimming for the bottom of a little girl's dress. 6½ inches wide, 1½ yards in the pattern. Dress 7837 comes in sizes 4 to 12 years. 15 cents each.

14312—This narrow floral border, ¾ inch wide, is appropriate for embroidering neckwear, underwear and children's clothes. It is illustrated on dress 8468, which comes in sizes 16, 17 and 18 years. 15 cents. Transfer pattern contains 6 yards of border for 10 cents.

14563—Flowered scalloped borders are pretty for finishing the edges of ruffles. This pattern is 1-inch wide and 6 yards and 4 corners are given for 10 cents. It is illustrated on dress 8584, which comes in sizes 16, 17 and 18 years. 15 cents.

14553—Scalloped borders give a firm finish to edges of sheer materials. This border, illustrated on child's dress, 8544, is ⅜-inch wide, 6 yards and 4 corners are given for 10 cents. The dress comes in sizes 8, 10, 12 and 14 years. 15 cents.

EMBROIDERED NÉGLIGÉES AND CAPS

14682—These flower sprays and scallops make an attractive finish for négligée 7413. There are 3 yards of each border in the pattern for 10 cents. The garment comes in sizes 34 to 42 inches. 15 cents.

14680—This border may be developed in cord or embroidery on négligée 8015, which is cut in sizes 32 to 44 inches. 15 cents. The border is 2 inches wide, 3 yards and 4 corners are given for 10 cents.

14690—The flowered scalloped border is 7 inches deep, and the plain scallops are ¾ inch deep. 2 yards of each are given in the pattern. They are illustrated on négligée 8441, which comes in sizes 32, 36, 40 and 44 inches. 15 cents each.

8071
Emb. 14663

8064
Emb. 14065
14679

8015
Emb. 14680

7413
Emb. 14682

8441
Emb. 14690

8071
Emb. 14519

14663—A simple scalloped border makes a substantial finish for collars, cuffs, underwear and dresses. This border is 1-inch wide, 6 yards and 4 corners are given for 10 cents. It is illustrated on the full-length négligée, 8071, which comes in sizes 32, 36, 40, 44 and 48 inches. 15 cents.

14679—Dainty design for embroidering a boudoir cap in solid work and French knots. Cutting pattern is included. 15 cents.

14065—Developed in solid work and eyelets, this border is suitable for trimming négligées and underwear. 1¼ inches wide, 6 yards. 10 cents. It is illustrated on garment 8064, which comes in 5 sizes. 15 cents.

14687—These flower sprays and beading may be used on négligées, underwear, neckwear or fancy articles, and should be developed in solid work, eyelets and French knots in white or colors. 10 cents. They are illustrated on dressing-sacque 8010, the pattern for which also contains the cutting outline for the boudoir cap. 15 cents.

14519—Developed in French knots, this border, 5 inches wide, makes an effective trimming for négligées and dresses of handkerchief linen, crêpe de Chine or chiffon. It is illustrated on négligée 8071. One and one-half yards of border are given for 10 cents.

8010
Emb. 14687

DESIGNS FOR HAND-EMBROIDERED LINGERIE

14568—Design for nightgown. This may be adapted to a slip-over or front-closing nightgown, chemise or combination garment. It is illustrated on garment 7267, which comes in sizes 32, 36, 40 and 44. 15 cents each.

14505—Scalloped border. 5½ inches wide and 2¼ yards. It may be embroidered in solid work and eyelets on petticoat 7740, which comes in 8 sizes, 22, 24, 26, 28, 30, 32, 34, 36. 15 cents each.

14463—Design for nightgown. Pattern includes front, back and sleeves. May be used with chemise design 14133, and border 14134, for embroidering a set of underwear. Illustrated on nightgown 7707, which comes in sizes 32, 36, 40 and 44. 15 cents each.

14493—Design for nightgown. Pattern includes transfers for stamping neck, back, front and sleeves. Illustrated on nightgown 7267, which is cut in 4 sizes, 32, 36, 40 and 44. 15 cents each.

14533—Border for trimming petticoats. 6½ inches wide, 1½ yards. Illustrated on petticoat 8105, which is cut in 7 sizes, 22 to 34. 15 cents each.

14655—French and eyelet design for empire nightgown. Pattern includes neck, sleeves and a strip of beading, which may be omitted if the loose gown is desired. Illustrated on garment 7267 which comes in 4 sizes. 15 cents each.

7267-14568

7267-14655

7740-14505

8105-14533

7077-14463

7267-14493

7254-14133-14134

7267-14637

7077-14271

8108-8111-14515

14133—Design for corset-cover or chemise, combined with border 14134, 4 inches wide, 2¼ yards, is illustrated on chemise 7254. Transfer patterns are 15 cents each. The chemise design, cut in sizes 32, 36 and 40 inches bust measure, is 10 cents.

14637—Nightgown design. May be cut from pattern 7267, which comes in 4 sizes. The large dots, in the embroidery, may be covered with small Irish roses, and directions for crocheting these are given on pattern envelope. 15 cents each.

14271—Wreaths and bow-knots for nightgown. To be embroidered in solid work, eyelets, outline and seed-stitch. An initial may be placed in the wreath. Illustrated on pattern 7077, cut in 4 sizes, 32, 36, 40 and 44 inches. 15 cents each.

14515—Beading design. 2¼ inches wide, 3 yards. Suitable for trimming underwear, dresses and négligée. Illustrated on chemise 8108, cut in sizes 32, 36, 40, 44, also on drawers 8111, cut in sizes 22, 24, 26, 30. 10 cents each.

DAINTY UNDERWEAR DESIGNS

14565—Design for combination garment. Pattern includes transfers for stamping corset-cover and two ruffles for drawers, each 42 inches long. May be adapted to chemise or nightgown, using ruffles for bottom of the skirt or sleeves. Illustrated on ladies' and misses' envelope combination 8033, sizes 32, 36, and 40. 15 cents each.

14567—Design for embroidering a combination garment. Pattern includes corset-cover and two ruffles for drawers, each 42 inches long. This design may also be adapted to a nightgown or chemise, and is illustrated on garment 7780, which is cut in sizes 32 to 42 inches bust measure. 15 cents each.

14536—Nightgown design. Pattern includes transfers for stamping the front, back, sleeves and neck-outline. This design should be embroidered in solid work and punched work, or outline and seed-stitch. It is illustrated on gown 7077, which is cut in sizes 32, 36, 40 and 44 inches bust measure. 15 cents each.

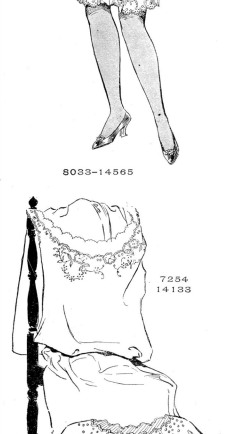

8033-14565

7780-14567

7077-14536

6148-14440-14239

7254
14133

7254-14554

6728-14509

8030-14408

14133—Design for corset-cover, chemise or combination garment. 15 cents. Border 14193, of same design, 2 inches wide, 3 yards, may be used with this. 10 cents. Illustrated on chemise 7254, cut in sizes 32, 36 and 40. 10 cents.

14408—Dotted scalloped border. 2½ inches wide, 3 yards and 4 corners. Makes a satisfactory finish for nightgowns, combinations and petticoats. 10 cents. Illustrated on nightgown 8030, which is cut in sizes 32, 36, 40 and 44 inches bust measure. 15 cents.

14509—Design for corset-cover and drawers. Pattern includes corset-cover and two ruffles, each 37 inches long. 10 cents. Illustrated on garment 6728, which comes in sizes 32, 36 and 40. 15 cents.

14440—Forget-me-not sprays. This design, combined with scalloped border with beading 14239, 1⅛ inches wide and 6 yards long, is illustrated on corset-cover 6148, which comes in sizes 32, 36, 40 and 44. 10 cents each.

14554—Design for chemise or corset-cover. To be embroidered in solid work and eyelet. 15 cents. Illustrated on garment 7254, which comes in sizes 32, 36 and 40. 10 cents.

DESIGNS FOR EMBROIDERING INFANTS' WEAR

14464—Infant's shoes. These pretty little shoes for the baby are very easy to embroider in solid work, on linen, broadcloth or flannel. The sole should be of a double thickness of the material. Cutting pattern is included. 10 cents.

14224—Infant's shoes. These little shoes may be made of broadcloth, linen or cashmere and embroidered in solid work in white. A cutting pattern is included, and directions for making are given on the pattern envelope. 10 cents.

14467—Design for infant's bonnet. Pattern also includes cutting outline and ends for strings. This design may be embroidered on handkerchief linen or broadcloth, in solid or eyelet work, in white. 10 cents.

14467—Design for infant's bonnet. 10 cents.

14048—Design for child's collar. Suitable for embroidering a deep collar or cape for an infant's long or short coat. 15 cents.

14638—Infant's bonnet. This bonnet is cut so that it can be very easily laundered, as when the strings are untied it can be spread out flat. This pattern is for a child from 1 to 1½ years old. 15 cents

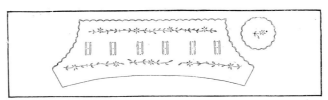

14564—Infant's bonnet. Nothing could be daintier than this little bonnet, for the new baby, embroidered in solid and eyelet work on handkerchief linen, and edged with Valenciennes lace. 10 cents.

14538—Two yoke designs for embroidering baby's first dresses, in solid work and eyelets, in white. 15 cents.

14208—Infant's bonnet. This pretty little bonnet may be embroidered on lawn, handkerchief linen or silk. Cutting pattern is included with the transfer pattern. 10 cents.

14538—Two yoke designs. To be developed in solid and eyelet work on a dress of fine lawn or handkerchief linen. 15 cents.

14168—Infant's circular sack. May be embroidered in solid work with filo silk on cashmere, albatross or fine French flannel. Cutting pattern included. 15 cents.

14639—Infant's sack. May be embroidered in white or a delicate pink or blue. The seams should be finished with cat-stitching, and the small collar may be omitted, if desired. 15 cents.

14326—Infant's sack. This square sack should be tied into shape with narrow wash ribbon. These may be taken out so that the sack is flat while being laundered. 15 cents.

ATTRACTIVE DESIGNS FOR BABY'S CLOTHES

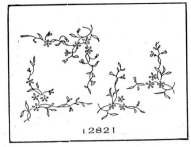

12821

14688

14695

14695

12820

12821—Forget-me-not spray suitable for embroidering infant's sack, bonnet or dress of very fine material. 10 cents.

14688—Infant's cap. An attractive cap may be made of handkerchief linen or lawn and embroidered with this simple design in eyelets and solid work. Ribbon should be run through the large eyelets to draw the cap into shape. 15 cents.

14538—Two designs for infant's yokes. These simple little yoke designs, embroidered in solid and eyelet work, are very dainty for trimming baby's first dresses of batiste, lawn or handkerchief linen. The wreath design is illustrated on dress 6344. 15 cents.

14636—Design for an infant's dress. This design, illustrated on bottom of dress 6344, may be embroidered in eyelets. Pattern includes yoke and sprays to be used on a dress for a child from six months to two years old. 10 cents.

12820—Forget-me-not design for a yoke to be embroidered in solid and eyelet work on infant's dress. 10 cents.

14695—Two designs for infant's bibs. These dainty little designs should be stamped on lawn or handkerchief linen and embroidered in solid work and eyelets. The bibs should be used over a padded quilting, just a little smaller than the bib. By omitting the scalloped edges these designs might be used for embroidering yokes of dresses. 15 cents.

14564—Infant's bonnet. For the cold months a little bonnet of blue or pink silk quilting may be slipped inside. This bonnet should be made of handkerchief linen and embroidered in white. 10 cents.

14635—Cape and collar for infant's coat. To be worked on cashmere, broadcloth or silk. Illustrated in coat 6577. 15 cents.

6344

Emb.
14538
14636

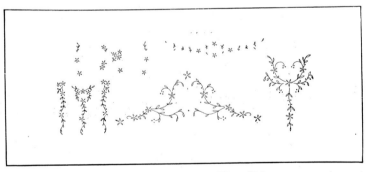

14442—Five designs for infant's dresses. These little sprays may be combined with tiny tucks or very narrow Valenciennes insertion. These designs may also be adapted to children's dress, neckwear and underwear of very fine material. 10 cents.

6577

Emb.
14564
14635

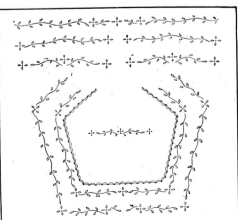

14636—Design for an infant's dress. The scallops forming the neck outline may be omitted on a high neck dress. 10 cents.

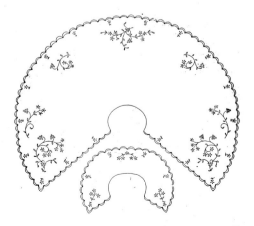

14635—Cape and collar for infant's coat. To be used on a long or short coat of cashmere, broadcloth, or corded silk. 15 cents.

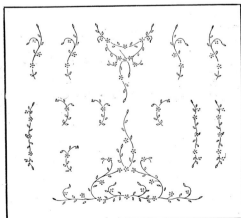

14627—Sheet of sprays. These sprays may be used on infant's long or short dresses, bonnets, sacks or petticoats. 10 cents.

FOR EMBROIDERING THE CHILDREN'S DRESSES

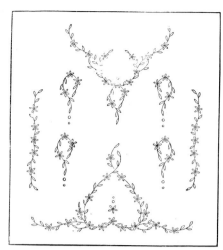

14286—These sprays are pretty for a little child's dress. Pattern includes yoke, panel for bottom of skirt, cuffs and motifs for scattering. 10 cents

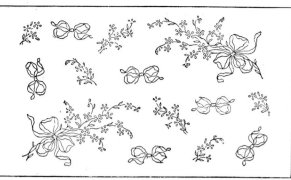

13448—These forget-me-not sprays are appropriate for use on neckwear, children's and infants' garments and fancy articles. 10 cents.

14196—Nine sprays in the pattern. These designs may be adapted in many ways to children's clothes, infant's garments, neckwear, underwear and blouses, and they may be embroidered in solid and eyelet work. These designs are particularly suitable for embroidering dresses of linen, chambray and lawn. 10 cents

14418—These 6 sprays may be adapted, developed in solid or eyelet work, to children's dresses, infant's garments, underwear or lingerie blouses. 10 cents

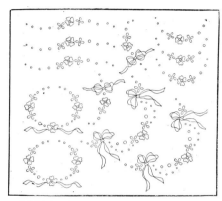

14089—To be embroidered in solid work, eyelets and seed-stitch. Border 14192 may be used with these sprays. 10 cents.

14440—These dainty little sprays may be carried out in solid work combined with outline and seeding on little dresses or aprons of linen, batiste, lawn or chambray. 10 cents.

14417—Five sprays in the pattern. These simple motifs may be embroidered in solid and eyelet work for trimming children's clothes, waists and underwear. 10 cents.

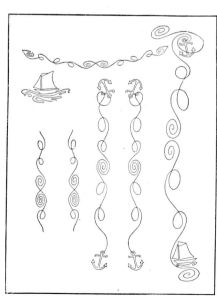

14254—Pattern includes collar, cuffs, belt and design for side-closing. This may be worked in outline-stitch in red, blue or white and is very attractive on a little boy's suit of serge or linen. 15 cents

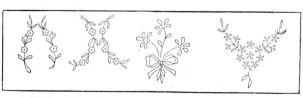

14109—Six transfers of each design. These may be adapted in many ways to children's or infant's dresses of linen or lingerie materials. 10 cents.

14064—The pattern includes three panels, each 4¼ inches wide by 15 inches long and 1¼ yards of border 1¾ inches wide. These may be embroidered in solid and eyelet work and may be adapted to dresses of linen or lingerie materials for the little girl or for her older sister. 15 cents

14250—Pattern includes back and front and motifs with eyelets for a belt. This may be embroidered in solid work and outline-stitch on a dress of linen or lingerie material. 15 cents.

BORDERS FOR UNDERWEAR AND HOUSEHOLD LINENS

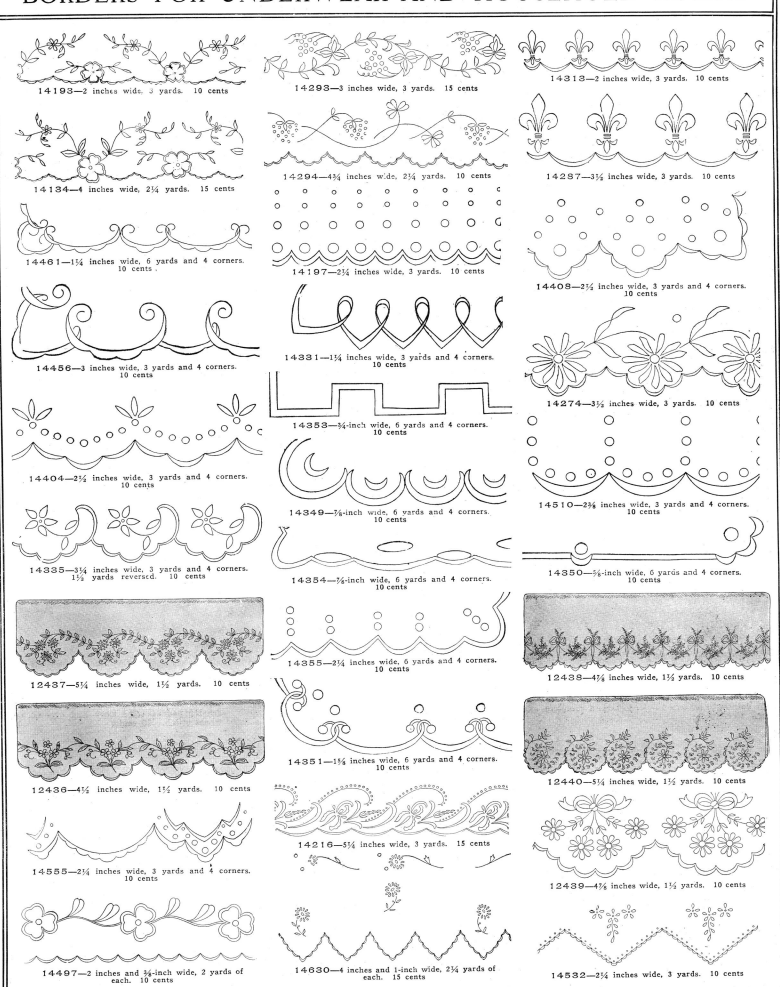

14193—2 inches wide, 3 yards. 10 cents

14134—4 inches wide, 2¼ yards. 15 cents

14461—1¼ inches wide, 6 yards and 4 corners.
10 cents

14456—3 inches wide, 3 yards and 4 corners.
10 cents

14404—2½ inches wide, 3 yards and 4 corners.
10 cents

14335—3¼ inches wide, 3 yards and 4 corners.
1½ yards reversed. 10 cents

12437—5¼ inches wide, 1½ yards. 10 cents

12436—4½ inches wide, 1½ yards. 10 cents

14555—2¼ inches wide, 3 yards and 4 corners.
10 cents

14497—2 inches and ⅜-inch wide, 2 yards of
each. 10 cents

14293—3 inches wide, 3 yards. 15 cents

14294—4¾ inches wide, 2¼ yards. 10 cents

14197—2¼ inches wide, 3 yards. 10 cents

14331—1¼ inches wide, 3 yards and 4 corners.
10 cents

14353—¾-inch wide, 6 yards and 4 corners.
10 cents

14349—⅞-inch wide, 6 yards and 4 corners.
10 cents

14354—⅞-inch wide, 6 yards and 4 corners.
10 cents

14355—2¼ inches wide, 6 yards and 4 corners.
10 cents

14351—1⅝ inches wide, 6 yards and 4 corners.
10 cents

14216—5¼ inches wide, 3 yards. 15 cents

14630—4 inches and 1-inch wide, 2¼ yards of
each. 15 cents

14313—2 inches wide, 3 yards. 10 cents

14287—3½ inches wide, 3 yards. 10 cents

14408—2½ inches wide, 3 yards and 4 corners.
10 cents

14274—3½ inches wide, 3 yards. 10 cents

14510—2⅜ inches wide, 3 yards and 4 corners.
10 cents

14350—⅝-inch wide, 6 yards and 4 corners.
10 cents

12438—4⅞ inches wide, 1½ yards. 10 cents

12440—5¼ inches wide, 1½ yards. 10 cents

12439—4⅞ inches wide, 1½ yards. 10 cents

14532—2¼ inches wide, 3 yards. 10 cents

DAINTY LUNCHEON SETS

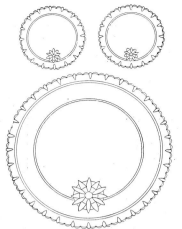

14694—Plate and tumbler doilies; 4 and 10 inches in diameter, 4 transfers of each in the pattern. 15 cents.

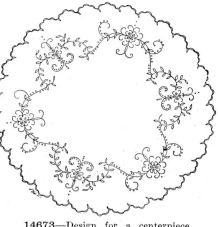

14673—Design for a centerpiece. 22 inches in diameter. To be worked in eyelets, outline-stitch, and solid work, in white. 15 cents.

14371—Copenhagen design for doily; 6¾ inches in diameter, 6 transfers in the pattern. This may be used with doily 14372, and centerpiece 14374. 15 cents.

14685—Design for between-meals mat. 22 inches in diameter. This may be developed in outline-stitch or long-and-short stitch. 15 cents.

14485—Grape design for a doily. 10½ inches in diameter, 4 transfers in the pattern. To be used with the grape centerpiece, 14317. 15 cents.

14691—Scalloped border. 4 inches wide. 3 yards of border, 1½ yards reversed 4 corners and 4 extra scallops. 15 cents.

14693—Design for centerpiece, 18 inches in diameter. This centerpiece may be used with the doilies, in pattern 14694, to form a complete set. 15 cents.

14659—Wheat design for centerpiece. 36 inches in diameter. Should be developed in heavily padded solid work and eyelets, or in wheat stitch. 15 cents.

14692

14669—Luncheon set. Pattern includes 25 pieces; 1 centerpiece, 36 inches in diameter; 8 doilies each of the 10-inch, 6-inch, and 4-inch size. This luncheon set should be embroidered in solid work, eyelets and outline-stitch in white. 15 cents.

14692—Motifs for a luncheon-cloth. Four motifs, each 8½ and 9 inches, and 12, each of 3¾ by 2¾ and 3¼ by 2 inches. The smaller motifs may be used on napkins or small doilies to form a set. 15 cents.

14672—Design for luncheon set. Pattern includes a luncheon-cloth, 36 inches square and 4 napkins, each 15½ inches square. Damask or fine round-thread linen may be used for this set, which should be developed in solid work, eyelets and outline-stitch. 15 cents.

14672

FLORAL CENTERPIECE AND DOILY DESIGNS

14368—Fruit design for centerpiece; 30 inches in diameter. To be done in punched work on heavy loosely-woven linen. 15 cents.

14162—Pineapple design for centerpiece; 20 inches in diameter. May be in white or colors on heavy round-thread linen. 15 cents.

13165—Centerpiece in modern Italian stitches; 22 inches in diameter. To be done in French laid and eyelet work or coronation braiding. 15 cents.

14459—American beauty rose centerpiece; 22 inches in diameter. May be worked in white or colors on white or tan linen. 15 cents.

14468—Elderberry centerpiece; 22 inches in diameter. To be worked in lazy-daisy stitch, French dots and outline-stitch. 15 cents.

14375—Design for centerpiece and two doilies; centerpiece 22 inches in diameter; doilies 12 and 6 inches in diameter. 15 cents.

14129— Oval eyelet doily; 9½ by 13½ inches; two transfers in the pattern. May be done in solid or eyelet work. 15 cents.

13626—Design for centerpiece in Roman cut-work; 23 inches in diameter. To be embroidered on heavy hand-woven linen. 15 cents.

14397—Design for an oval doily; size 16¼ by 22 inches. May be done in solid work and shadow eyelets. 15 cents.

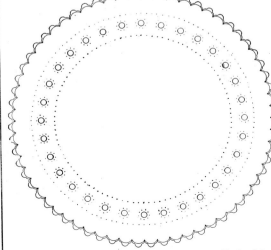

14577—Centerpiece; 22 inches in diameter. To be done in solid work and French knots on linen. 15 cents.

13664—Design for a tan linen centerpiece, to be used on bare polished tables; 22 inches in diameter. 15 cents.

13040—Conventional design for eyelet centerpiece; 22 inches in diameter. 15 cents.

SIMPLE DESIGNS FOR BED-ROOM LINENS

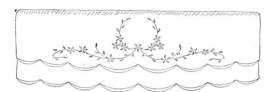

14543—Transfers for stamping both ends of 3 guest-towels are included in the pattern. Each design is 18 inches long and should be developed in white. 1-inch initials or monograms may be placed in the wreath. These designs are also very pretty for embroidering pillow-slips. 15 cents.

14634—For embroidering heavy huckaback towels for general use, simple scallop designs such as these are most practical. Pattern includes scalloping for finishing both ends of 3 towels. Each 22 inches long. An initial or monogram may be placed in the center above the scalloping. 15 cents.

14561—These 3 guest-towels should be developed in colors in darning, punched work and outline-stitch. These designs are suitable for 18-inch or 15-inch huckaback. The motifs in these designs may be used for embroidering bureau scarfs, pincushions, collar bags and laundry bags. 10 cents.

12780—Sprays for pillow-cases or sheet. 4 transfers, each 6 by 11 inches. 15 cents.

14294—Border for set of bed-room linens. 4¾ inches wide, 2¼ yards in the pattern. 10 cents.

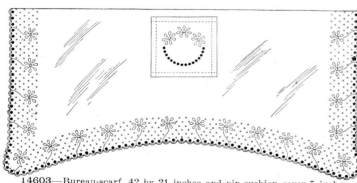

14603—Bureau-scarf, 42 by 21 inches and pin-cushion cover 5 inches in diameter. 15 cents.

14188—Design for bureau-scarf and pin-cushion or curtains. 4 medallions each 6 by 6 inches and 2 yards of border 2¼ inches wide. 15 cents.

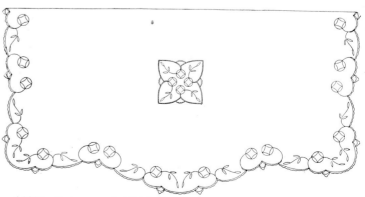

14604—The bureau-scarf is 19 by 41 inches and a pin-cushion cover 7 inches square. 15 cents.

14601—Bureau-scarf, 41½ inches long by 22 inches wide, pin-cushion 5 inches square. 15 cents.

FOR TOWELS, SHEETS AND BUREAU-SCARFS

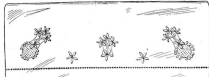

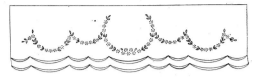

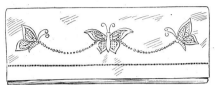

14656—Designs for guest-towels, each 18 inches long. 3 designs in the pattern. 10 cents.

14629—Three designs for guest-towels, each 18 inches long. 10 cents.

14696—Three guest-towels, each 18 inches long. To be developed in colors. 15 cents.

14091—For solid or eyelet embroidery to be adapted to pillow-cases or bureau-scarfs. For stamping both ends of two towels. 24 inches long. 10 cents.

14559—Transfer for stamping both ends of two towels, pillow-cases or bureau-scarfs are included in the pattern. 22 inches long. 10 cents.

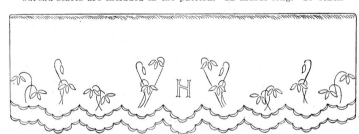

14332—Simple design for a large towel Transfers for both ends of two towels. 22 inches long. Initial taken from pattern 14140. Each 10 cents.

14334—A pretty snow-drop design for eyelet work on fine huckaback. Transfers for ends of two towels on 22-inch material. 10 cents.

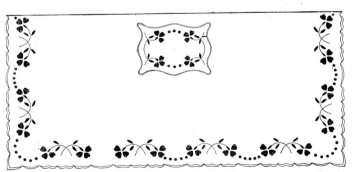

14633—Designs for sheet and pillow-cases. Sheet, 56 by 3½ inches, and 2 transfers for pillow-cases, each 16¾ by 3½ inches. 15 cents.

14602—Design for a bureau-scarf and pin-cushion cover. Bureau-scarf, 18 by 42 inches, pin-cushion cover, 5½ by 7½ inches. 15 cents.

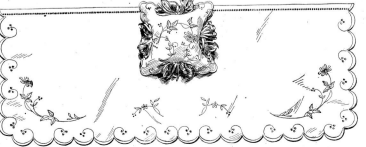

14457—Grape design for sideboard-cover, 18 by 42 inches. By using two patterns, a luncheon-cloth 36 inches square can be made. 15 cents.

14631—Bureau-scarf, 40½ by 16½ inches and pin-cushion cover to match 7¾ inches square. 15 cents.

PATTERN 14528 INCLUDES 375 TRANSFERS OF ONE INITIAL IN ALL THESE STYLES AND SIZES FOR 15 CENTS

For Marking Sets of Linens

Showing monograms CB made by overlapping the flowered letters from pattern 14528. The flowers and leaves may be embroidered in white or colors in solid work.

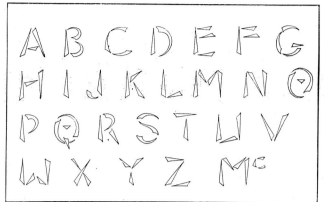

14677—Alphabet in Japanese style. 3 sizes in one pattern; ¾-inch, 1½ inches and 2¼ inches high. Suitable for embroidering household linens and fancy articles in solid work or outline and seed-stitch. 10 cents.

Monogram DE formed by the fancy script letters from pattern 14528. These letters are suitable for marking dining-room or bed-room linens in white.

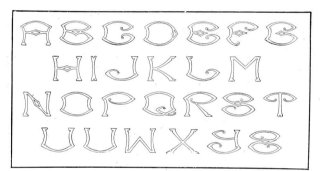

14528—Wide Gothic letters 3¼, 2¼ and 1½ inches high. 6 of 3¼-inch size and 12 each of 2¼ and 1½-inch sizes

Showing monogram made by combining wide and narrow Gothic letters

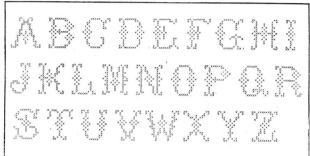

14528—Cross-stitch letters in 1½ and 3-inch sizes. 12 of each size of one initial

14528—Slanted letters; right and left and straight letters in this style in ½, ¾, 1½ and 2-inch sizes. 12 of each size

14528—Fancy script letters in 1, 1¾, 3 and 4-inch sizes. 6 of 3 and 4-inch sizes; 12 of 1 and 1¾-inch sizes

14528—Block letters in ½, ¾, 1 and 2-inch sizes; 12 of each size

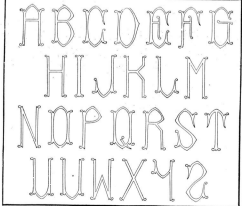

14528—Plain script letters, 1, 2, 3¼ and 4 inches high. 6 of 3¼ and 4-inch sizes; 12 of 1 and 2-inch sizes

14528—Narrow Gothic letters in 4½, 3¼ and 2¼-inch sizes. 6 each of 4½ and 3¼-inch sizes; 12 of 2¼-inch size

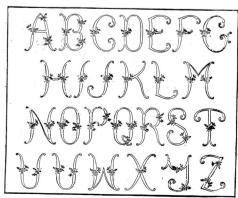

14528—Flowered letters, 1, 2, 3 and 4 inches high. 6 each of 3 and 4-inch sizes; 12 1 and 2-inch sizes

STANDARD INITIALS AND ALPHABETS FOR EMBROIDERY

No. 14068—Script Initial Letters, forty-two letters, five sizes of any one letter in one pattern. 12 of the ½-inch and 1-inch sizes, 6 each of the 2-inch, 3-inch and 4-inch sizes. Any monogram may be formed by placing these letters so that they slightly overlap. 10 cents.

No. 14066—Old English Initial Letters, forty-two letters, five sizes of any one letter in one pattern. 12 of the ½-inch size, 12 of the 1-inch size, 6 of the 2-inch size, 6 of the 3-inch size, 6 of the 4-inch size. 10 cents.

14306—Script Alphabet. A complete alphabet in 6-inch size only. For blankets, bedspreads and robes. Any monogram can be formed by placing these letters so that they slightly overlap. 15 cents.

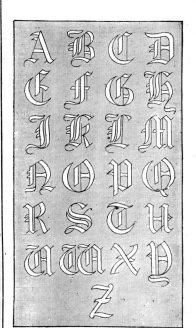

No. 14484—Old English Initials. Forty-two letters, five sizes of any one letter in one pattern. 12 of the ½-inch size, 12 of the 1-inch size, 6 of the 2-inch size, 6 of the 3-inch size, 6 of the 4-inch size. 10 cents.

No. 14454—Cross-stitch Alphabet. Includes a complete alphabet in 2-inch, 3-inch or 4-inch size. Suitable for towels, blankets or other household linens. 10 cents.

No. 14266—Block Initials. Fifty-four letters, six sizes of any one letter in one pattern. 12 of the ⅜-inch size, 12 of the ½-inch size, 12 of the 1-inch size, 6 of the 2-inch size, 6 of the 3-inch size and 6 of the 4-inch size in one pattern. 10 cents.

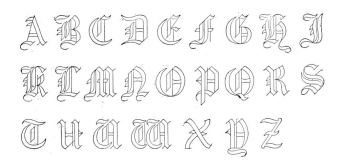

No. 14140—Old English Alphabet in 1-inch, 2-inch or 3-inch size. A complete alphabet in any one size in one pattern. 10 cents.

No. 14230—Script Alphabet in 1-inch, 2-inch, 3-inch or 4-inch size. A complete alphabet in any one size in one pattern. 10 cents.

THE CORRECT PLACING AND WORKING OF INITIALS

14528

14528

14528

The cross-stitch letters are especially suitable for towels of huckaback and they should be worked so that there will be no right and wrong side to the embroidery. This can be done with a little practice by working all the under stitches to run in one direction, then going over the design with the cross-stitches running in the opposite direction. The cross-stitch letters may be used on turkish towels by basting the transfer pattern to the material and working over the paper which may be torn away.

THE CORRECT SIZES TO USE

For table-cloths, 4-inch letters; for lunch or tea-cloths, 3-inch initials or monogram. On centerpieces, 2-inch letters, and 1-inch letters on doilies, tray-cloths and platter-cloths. 2 or 3-inch letters may be used on sideboard-scarfs.

For marking guest-towels use 1-inch letters, and for large towels, 2 or 3-inch letters. On sheets use

14528—Showing the overlapping of letters to form monograms.

4-inch initials, and on pillow-cases, 3-inch initials or 2-inch monograms. 4 or 6-inch letters may be used on blankets.

THE PLACING OF INITIALS AND MONOGRAMS

on the various articles on which they may be used depends on the personal preference of the worker and on the finish or decoration of the article itself. However, on some of the more common articles for household use it has become customary to place the initials in particular places and to use approximately uniform sizes.

For embroidering a monogram on a square table-cloth, stamp the letters in one corner about five inches from each hem. On a round table-cloth the letters may be placed either in the center or so that they will fall two inches over the edge of the table when the cloth is in use. For marking napkins, place the letters so that when the napkin is folded four times the letters will be in the center of the outside fold.

MATERIALS FOR WORKING. For working monograms and initials on bed-room linens, dining-room linens and any articles of cotton or linen material use mercerized cotton number 35 for one-half, three-fourths and one-inch letters; number 25 for two-inch letters and number 20 for three and four-inch sizes.

For embroidering initials or monograms on articles made from silk or wool materials use filo silk for the small letters and rope silk for the four-inch letters. Mercerized cotton is often used to embroider woolen articles which will be laundered, as blankets and crib-covers; but heavy rope silk is more satisfactory. The padding should be done with fine, soft padding cotton, as this does not separate or crack in washing as more firmly twisted grades sometimes do. Several strands may be used in the needle for padding the large letters.

Cross-stitch letters should be worked in mercerized cotton No. 5 or 7 for the large letters, and No. 12 for the smaller size.

STITCHES FOR EMBROIDERING INITIALS AND MONOGRAMS

The originality of the worker may suggest an unlimited variety of stitches for embroidering initials and monograms. The stitches used must depend somewhat on the material and the decoration of the article on which the letters are used. Well padded, solid embroidery is perhaps the simplest and most popular method used and this is suitable for working a monogram of any style on any material. The padding of the letters should be done very firmly and smoothly with soft padding cotton. First go over the stamped lines with fine outline-stitch, then fill in the spaces with coarser outline-stitches, taking a long stitch on the top of the material and a short one on the under side so that all the padding will lie on the right side of the material and the under side will be flat.

Very often the first and last initials of a monogram are worked in solid embroidery, and the center letter is carried out in outline-stitch, filling in the spaces with fine seed-stitch, Bermuda fagoting or punched embroidery.

For embroidering towels and blankets the letters are sometimes outlined and the spaces are filled in with French dots. When a monogram is to be combined with a design worked in eyelets or Richelieu embroidery the wide parts of the letters may be worked in fine eyelets or in ladder work.

The placing of initials and monograms on small dining-room linens is determined largely by the shape and finish of the pieces. On square centerpieces and plate-doilies the letters are usually placed in one corner, while on round linens they may be placed in the center or near the edge. On a bedspread the monogram should be placed in the center; on a bureau-scarf the letters may be at one end, or two inches from the hem at the center of the scarf. Sheets should be stamped so that the monogram will be right side up when the end of the sheet is turned over. The letters may be placed in the center of the end two inches from the hem. Pillow-cases should be marked at the center of one end, two inches from the hem or scallop. Towels, if finished with hemstitching, may be marked one inch from the top of the hem, although this placing may be varied as suggested by the width of the hem or pattern of the material.

For embroidering initials or monograms on automobile blankets, the letters should be placed about three inches from the edge in one corner. On a baby carriage-robe, the monogram may be placed in the center, or in the center of the flap. For marking a blanket, stamp the letters three inches from the binding in the center of one end, placing them so that they will be right side up when the end of the blanket is turned over, as on the sheets.

On a man's shirt the initial or monogram is usually placed five inches above the cuff on the left sleeve; on shirtwaists the letters may be placed on the pocket or five inches below the shoulder on the left sleeve. For marking stockings, the monograms may be placed over the insteps, while on nightgowns and underwear they are usually embroidered in the center of the front. Sets of linens as table-cloth and napkins or sheet and pillow-cases of the same pattern and design should be marked with letters of the same style, but many like to use different styles for different sets.

It is now customary to mark all household linens with the initial or monogram of the "Lady of the house." A bride marks her trousseau with her initials, and gifts to a bride should also be marked with the initials of her maiden name.

A married woman embroiders her household linens with a monogram composed of the initial of her first name, the first initial of her maiden surname and the initial of her husband's surname.

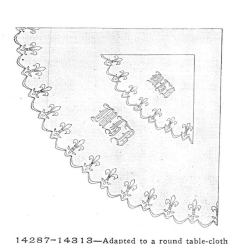

14287—14313—Adapted to a round table-cloth and napkin. The monograms are formed from two sizes of the block initials 14066.

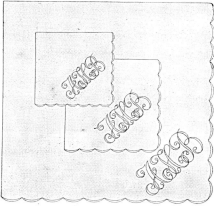

14153—Used for scalloping a table-cloth. The napkins are scalloped with 14301 and table-cloth with 14153. Monograms are made from pattern 14068.

14068—Showing the correct placement of a monogram on a handkerchief.

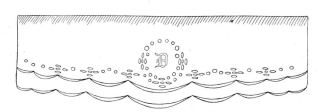

14484—Old English initials are always in style. This shows a single letter enclosed in the wreath in towel design 14127.

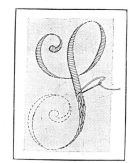

14068—Showing a letter in solid work.

DAINTY WREATH DESIGNS FOR ENCLOSING
INITIALS AND MONOGRAMS

14662—These wreaths are appropriate for inclosing 3-inch initials or 2-inch monograms, 1-inch initials or ½-inch monograms on household linens and novelties. The pattern includes 6 of each for 10 cents.

14416—1 wreath 7¼ by 5 inches; 6 wreaths 3¾ by 2¾ inches, 12 wreaths 2 by 1½ inches. For inclosing 1, 2 and 3-inch initials. 10 cents.

14661—The larger wreaths in this pattern are appropriate for inclosing 4-inch initials, or 3-inch monograms, while the smaller wreaths may be used to inclose 2-inch initials, or 1-inch monograms on household linens. The pattern includes 6 of each size for 15 cents.

14491—Two designs of wreaths each 5 inches in diameter. For 2-inch initials or monograms. 6 of each in the pattern for 10 cents

14204—Two designs for enclosing initials. 6 transfers of each in the pattern. Suitable for one-inch monograms on small table linens, underwear, guest-towels, bags, pin-cushions and card-cases. 10 cents.

14652—Pattern contains 4 wreaths, each 3½ inches in diameter, also pin-cushion cover, picture frame, 2 candle-shades and 5 napkin-rings. 15 cents.

13428—Two designs each 1¾ inches in diameter for inclosing 1-inch initials or ½-inch monograms. 12 of each for 10 cents

14231—Wreaths and flowers. Suitable for embroidering handkerchiefs, neckwear and infants' clothes. 1⅝ inches deep, 3 yards in pattern. ½-inch initial may be enclosed in wreath. 15 cents.

14139—Wreath and bow-knot design, 4¼ by 3½ inches. Suitable for enclosing a ½-inch initial. The pattern also contains 3 book covers. 10 cents.

14666—Wedgewood designs. Large wreath, 5 inches in diameter, 2 small wreaths, each 1½ by 2 inches, and a number of other designs. 15 cents.

12709—Wreath 9½ by 10 inches for inclosing a 4-inch letter or monogram. 10 cents

14124—Wreath for enclosing 2-inch monogram. 6 transfers given, 10 cents. Pattern 14126 includes six transfers of this design suitable for enclosing 4-inch initial or 3-inch monogram. 15 cents.

14085—Four designs of wreaths. Suitable for ½, ¾ and 1-inch letters. 6 of each in the pattern for 10 cents

STENCIL DESIGNS FOR HOUSEHOLD DECORATION

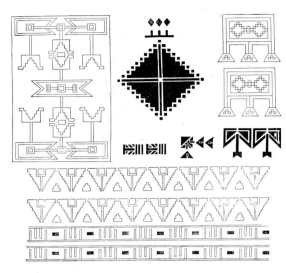

14654—Indian designs for embroidery and stenciling. They are to be worked in solid work on runners, pillows and dresses, book-covers, curtains and bags. Price 15 cents.

14620—Chinese Motifs. These attractive Chinese designs are appropriate for use on waists, dresses and suits. Price 15 cents.

14530—Three designs for patchwork. Sunflower design 12½ by 21¼ inches, pansy design 8½ by 7 inches, wild rose design 7 by 3 inches. They may be used on sofa-pillows, quilts or baby carriage-covers. Price 15 cents.

14474—Morning glory and dogwood designs for patchwork. They should be transferred to a piece of white cotton cloth to be used as a foundation when basting the design. Price 15 cents.

14450—Conventional Rose design for corner. Size 9 by 9 inches. 4 transfers in the pattern. It may be used for embroidering sofa-pillows, table-covers, bureau-scarfs, runners and screens. This design might also be used on a dress. Price 15 cents.

14159—Stencil designs for candle shades. Seven designs in the pattern. When lined with colored silk or Japanese paper these are very attractive. Price 15 cents.

14159—Includes seven designs for 15 cents.

14431—Three stencil designs. Lamp-shade is 14 inches wide at the bottom, 5⅜ inches wide at the top and 8 inches high; the two borders are 2 inches wide and 3 inches wide respectively. Price 15 cents.

14386—Three designs for patchwork. Fleur de lis design 9¾ by 6 inches. Basket design 9½ by 14½ inches. Border 12⅜ by 5¾ inches. They may be used on sofa-pillows or quilts. Price 15 cents.

14316—Six stencil designs. These designs may be used for stenciling lamp-shades, shirt-waist boxes, curtains, portieres, and pillows. Crafts canvas, Russian crash, Japanese grass cloth, scrim, burlap, linen and pongee are all suitable materials. Price 15 cents.

14613—Four stencil designs. Allover design is 15 by 12 inches; tulip border, 4½ inches wide; daisy border, 6 inches wide with corner 8¾ inches square and rose border, 3 inches wide. Price 15 cents.

ATTRACTIVE STENCILS FOR LIVING-ROOM DRAPERIES

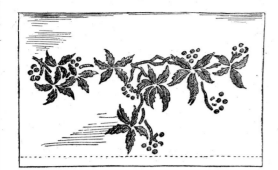

14298—Woodbine design, 10 by 17 inches. Suitable for stenciling or embroidering runners and portières in outline and darning-stitch or long-and-short stitch. Price 15 cents.

14362—Foliage designs for stencils. These designs are suitable for stenciling curtains, runners, bureau-scarfs and table-covers. Price 15 cents.

14169—Design for between-meals-mat. Size 23 by 40 inches. This may be developed in stencil or embroidery. Price 15 cents.

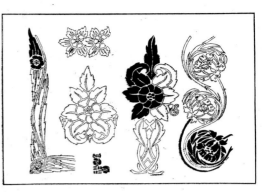

14339—Six designs for stenciling. For decorating curtains, portières, table-covers, sofa-pillows, screens, runners and novelties. Two or more colors may be used, in developing these designs, and, if desired, they may be outlined. Price 15 cents.

14336—Five stencil designs. These motifs may be used to form all-over patterns or borders on runners, pillows and curtains. Price 15 cents.

14660—Seven stencil designs. They may be used on runners, bureau-scarfs, curtains and pillows. Price 15 cents.

14118—Five stencil designs. The jonquil design illustrated on a laundry bag, is 10½ inches high. These designs may be used on runners, pillows and screens. Price 15 cents.

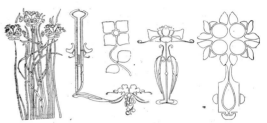

14299

14299—Seven stencil designs for decorating curtains, table-covers, pillows and runners. The tulip design on the runner is 13¾ by 11 inches. Price 15 cents.

14343—Nasturtium stencil. May be used on bed-spread, curtains and pillows. Border 3½ inches wide and spray 10½ by 36 inches. Price 15 cents.

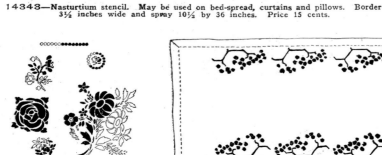

14365—Flower designs for stencils. May be used as all-over patterns or to form borders. Price 15 cents.

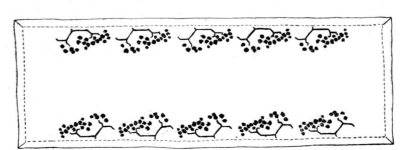

14112—Border for stencil or appliqué. 2¼ yards in the pattern. This stencil may be used effectively on drapery of linen scrim or pongee, or sofa pillows, table-covers, runners and bags. Price 15 cents.

14365—Flower designs for stencils. These designs are suitable for stenciling or block-printing, curtains, dresses and bedroom draperies. Price 15 cents.

CROSS-STITCH DIAGRAM PATTERNS TO BE WORKED OVER CROSS-STITCH CANVAS

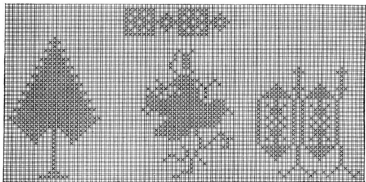

Diagram patterns to be worked on towels, runners and bags.

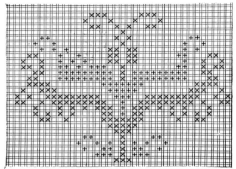

Diagram for cross-stitch motif to be used on a table-cover, or pillow.

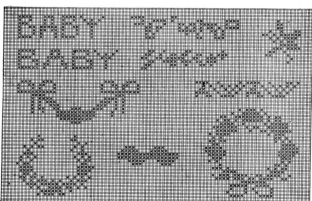

Cross-stitch diagrams to be used on towels and fancy articles.

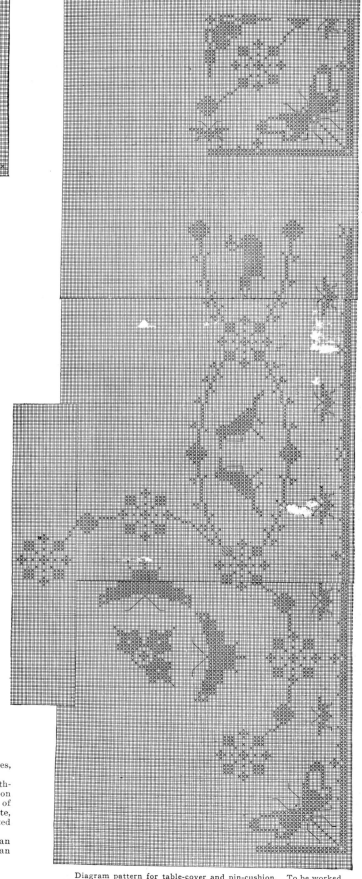

Diagram pattern for table-cover and pin-cushion. To be worked over cross-stitch canvas. This gives one-half of the corner design, and one-fourth of the pin-cushion.

HOW TO USE THE DIAGRAM PATTERNS.

These diagrams are to be used as patterns for working the designs over cross-stitch cambric. Each square on the diagram represents a square on the cambric. Baste a piece of cross-stitch canvas, a little more than three times the size of the diagram for the table-cover and pin-cushion, in place on your material, then by counting the squares you can easily work out the pattern in any colors you wish to use. For the smaller diagrams cut the canvas twice the size of the diagram. The borders may be repeated to any length.

These small diagrams are also appropriate for embroidering towels and cases for toilet articles. You will need No. 5 mercerized cotton in two shades of pink, two shades of light blue and a soft, grey green for developing these motifs and the rose design, and two shades of green for the tree. The border repeats can be developed in any colors you may choose.

No transfer patterns can be supplied, as these diagrams are patterns in themselves, and the designs are so simple that you will not need any other guide.

The cross-stitch cambric comes in three grades, coarse for heavy materials, as bath-towels, wash-cloths, baby carriage-covers and crib-covers; medium for general use on towels, table-covers and any articles of medium-weight fabrics, while the finest grade of this canvas should be used for embroidering little dresses, bonnets and aprons of batiste, handkerchief linen, dimity and other fine, sheer fabrics, using number 12 mercerized cotton for these sheer materials.

This cambric comes from 24 to 30 inches wide, at about thirty cents a yard, and can be purchased in any large department store at the art embroidery counter, or from an art embroidery specialty shop.

THE CROSS-STITCH DIAGRAM IN COLOR ON THE BACK COVER.*

These cross-stitch motifs and borders are appropriate for embroidering towels, bureau-scarfs, pillows, children's dresses, infants' garments and many pretty novelties for Christmas. No transfer patterns can be supplied for these designs.

*Now shown in black and white on page 89.

Description on page 88

[original inside back cover]

SUGGESTIONS FOR EMBROIDERING DRESS-TRIMMINGS

14641

14619

14644

14599

14600

14446

14579

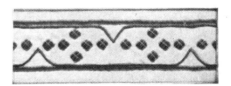

14598

14616

14508

14620

14482

14597

14589

14569

14609

14607

14446—This thousand-flower border is a most attractive trimming for a gown of marquisette or crêpe voile. It is 2¼ inches wide and includes 3 yards for 10 cents.

14482—This border may be developed in braid, cord or couching. It is 1¾ inches wide and includes 3 yards and 4 corners for 10 cents.

14508—This motif may be developed in braid or cord for trimming wraps or dresses. It is 4½ by 3 inches and 6 transfers are included for 10 cents.

14569—This may be developed in solid work or lazy-daisy-stitch. It is 1½ inches wide and 6 yards are included for 10 cents.

14579—These motifs, developed in braid or cord, make a smart trimming for a coat or dress. 10 cents.

14589—Developed in rope silk or wool, this is a most attractive trimming. It is 2 inches wide and includes 3 yards and 4 corners for 10 cents.

14597—This may be developed in braid or cord and combined with embroidery. It is 1½ inches wide and includes 3 yards and 4 corners for 10 cents.

14598—This border is pretty for children's clothes. It is 1½ inches wide and includes 3 yards and 4 corners for 10 cents.

14599—These flowers may be used in a border or scattered. The border is 2¾ inches wide and includes 3 yards for 10 cents.

14600—This is 2¼ inches wide and the pattern includes 3 yards for 10 cents.

14607—This pattern includes three narrow Bulgarian borders, 3 yards and 4 corners of each for 10 cents.

14609—Developed in Bulgarian colors, these motifs give a smart note to a dark costume. 15 cents.

14616—An attractive trimming for children's clothes. It is 1-inch wide and includes 6 yards for 10 cents.

14619—A smart, effective trimming for an evening gown or wrap, 4 in the pattern. 15 cents.

14620—These Chinese motifs are most attractive on dresses of crêpy materials. 17 in the pattern. 15 cents.

14641—The Futurist designs are the fad of the season, and this border is 2½ inches wide, 3 yards. 10 cents.

14644—This attractive border, also Futurist, is **very** smart. 2 inches wide, 3 yards for 10 cents.

[original back cover]